Mary's Day—Saturday

Meditations for Marian Celebrations

Mark G. Boyer

A Liturgical Press Book

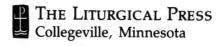

THE LITURGICAL PRESS
Collegeville, Minnesota

Cover design by Fred Petters

1	2	3	4	5	6	7	8	9

Library of Congress Cataloging-in-Publication Data

Boyer, Mark G.
    Mary's day—Saturday : meditations for Marian celebrations / Mark G. Boyer
        p.   cm.
    Includes bibliographical references.
    ISBN 0-8146-2092-2
    1. Mary, Blessed Virgin, Saint—Prayer-books and devotions—English. 2. Mary, Blessed Virgin, Saint—Feasts. 3. Church year meditations. I. Title. II. Title: Saturday.
BX2161.5.S26B69   1993
242'.74—dc20   92-39441
                                                                      CIP

Dedicated to the McEvoys

Jon and Jan,
Greg,
Suzy,
and Julie.

"Mary's life should be for you a pictorial image. . . . Her life is like a mirror reflecting the face of chastity and the form of virtue. Therein you may find a model for your own life, . . . showing what to improve, what to imitate, what to hold fast to."

—St. Ambrose of Milan, 339–397 A.D.
from "The Virgins" (377 A.D.)

Contents

Introduction

This book is titled *Mary's Day—Saturday: Meditations for Marian Celebrations*. After a brief introduction to post-Vatican II Mariology in chapter 1, chapter 2 provides a prayerful exercise for each Marian celebration during the liturgical year. During its annual cycle the Church celebrates fourteen different days in honor of the Blessed Virgin Mary: three solemnities, three feasts, four memorials, and four optional memorials.

In the course of the life of the Church there also developed the custom of keeping Saturday as Mary's Day. "The custom of dedicating Saturday to the Blessed Virgin Mary arose in Carolingian monasteries at the end of the eighth century and soon spread throughout Europe."[1] It did not take long for special Mass formularies in honor of the Blessed Virgin Mary to be written and to be incorporated into the liturgical books. In fact, "in the liturgical reform following the Council of Trent, the custom of celebrating a memorial of the Blessed Virgin Mary on Saturday was incorporated into the *Missale Romanum*."[2]

The bishops of Vatican Council II did not abandon this practice of observing a memorial of Mary on Saturday. Rather, they clarified its meaning and made possible more frequent celebrations by increasing the number of Masses and biblical readings. The directive in the "General Instruction of the Roman Missal" concerning Masses in honor of the Blessed Virgin Mary on Saturday reflects this perspective: "On Saturdays in Ordinary Time when there is no obligatory memorial, an optional memorial of the Blessed Virgin Mary is allowed."[3]

In 1986, in honor of the most recent Marian Year, a *Collection of Masses of the Blessed Virgin Mary* was issued by the Congregation for Divine Worship in Rome. The General Introduction to these forty-six Masses further emphasizes the importance of celebrating "the memorial of the Blessed Virgin on Saturday as a kind of introduction to the Lord's Day."[4] As people "prepare to celebrate

1

the weekly remembrance of the Lord's resurrection" on Sunday, they "look with great reverence to the Blessed Virgin, who, alone of all his disciples, on that 'great Sabbath' when Christ lay in the tomb, kept watch with full faith and hope and awaited his resurrection."[5]

Besides Saturdays in Ordinary Time, for "the spiritual benefit of the faithful,"[6] a Mass in honor of the Blessed Virgin Mary may be celebrated on any day when the choice of a Mass is open. According to the "General Introduction" to the *Collection of Masses of the Blessed Virgin Mary,* however, "priests and faithful should keep in mind that genuine Marian devotion does not demand the multiplication of Masses of the Blessed Virgin."[7]

Chapter 3 contains a prayerful exercise for each of the forty-six Masses found in the *Collection of Masses of the Blessed Virgin Mary.* These Masses are divided among the liturgical seasons of Advent, Christmas, Lent, Easter, and Ordinary Time.

This book is designed to be used by individuals for private prayer and by homilists for public preaching. For each Marian celebration a five-part exercise is presented.

1. In chapter 2 a few short verses of Scripture are taken from one of the readings provided in the Lectionary for Mass of each solemnity, feast, memorial, or optional memorial of the Blessed Virgin Mary during the liturgical year. When there are no assigned readings, one has been chosen from the Common of the Blessed Virgin Mary in the Lectionary. A list of these texts can be found in the Appendix.

In chapter 3 a few short verses of Scripture are taken from one of the readings provided for each of the forty-six Masses found in the *Collection of Masses of the Blessed Virgin Mary: Lectionary.* On any Saturday the reader may choose a reflection from the appropriate season. The numbering and the title for each Mass found in the *Collection of Masses of the Blessed Virgin Mary* has been retained in this book.

2. All of the Scriptures assigned for the particular solemnity, feast, memorial, optional memorial, or Mass are given. In this way, the reader can examine the connection between the readings for a given Marian celebration.

3. A reflection follows which attempts to expand an idea or an image found in the verses from the Scripture and the particular Mar-

ian celebration. It can be used as the starter for a homily or it can easily be considered as a homilette in itself.

4. The reflection is followed by a question for personal meditation. The question functions as a guide for further development of the idea or image chosen in the reflection. The homilist can use the question to develop a homily or pose it to the congregation for reflection. After the question a suitable period of silence should be allowed for meditation.

5. A prayer summarizes the original theme of the Scripture. The prayer can conclude the exercise for the individual, or it can be used as a fitting conclusion to the General Intercessions and the Liturgy of the Word during the celebration of the Eucharist.

It is the author's hope that this book will foster authentic devotion to the mother of God and "her close participation in the history of salvation."[8] The reader should remember that "when the Church commemorates the role of the Mother of the Lord in the work of redemption or honors her privileges, it is above all celebrating the events of salvation in which, by God's salvific plan, the Blessed Virgin was involved in view of the mystery of Christ."[9]

Notes

1. "General Introduction," *Collection of Masses of the Blessed Virgin Mary* (hereafter CMBVM) (Collegeville, Minn.: The Liturgical Press, 1992) par. 35.

2. Ibid.

3. "General Instruction of the Roman Missal," Liturgy Documentary Series 2 (Washington, D.C.: United States Catholic Conference, 1982) par. 15.

4. CMBVM, par. 36.

5. Ibid.

6. Ibid., par. 37.

7. Ibid.

8. Ibid., par. 6.

9. Ibid.

Chapter I

A Brief Mariology

Chapter 8 of the "Dogmatic Constitution on the Church" of Vatican II devotes eighteen paragraphs to Mariology under the title "Our Lady." The fathers of the council make it clear that they do not "intend to give a complete doctrine on Mary" nor do they "wish to decide those questions which the work of theologians has not yet fully clarified."[1]

The fathers of the council insist that Mary "occupies a place in the Church which is the highest after Christ and also closest to us."[2] Furthermore, "the Church does not hesitate to profess this subordinate role of Mary, which it constantly experiences and recommends to the heartfelt attention of the faithful, so that encouraged by this maternal help they may the more closely adhere to the Mediator and Redeemer."[3]

A sound Mariology flows out of a firm Christology, is grounded in a solid ecclesiology, and is intimately united with a steadfast theology of the communion of saints. The "General Introduction" of the *Collection of Masses of the Blessed Virgin Mary,* issued in 1986 by the Congregation for Divine Worship for the most recent Marian Year, makes this clear when it states that this collection of Masses "seeks to promote celebrations that are marked by sound doctrine, the rich variety of their themes, and their rightful commemoration of the saving deeds that the Lord God has accomplished in the Blessed Virgin in view of the mystery of Christ and the Church."[4]

1) Mariology Flows from Christology

"Mary is . . . closely linked with the mystery of Christ,"[5] the "General Introduction" declares. "In celebrating the mystery of Christ, the Church also frequently and with deep reverence honors

5

the Blessed Virgin Mary, because of her close bonds with her Son,"[6] state Augustin Cardinal Mayer and Archbishop Virgilio Noe in the Congregation for Divine Worship Decree that accompanies the *Collection of Masses of the Blessed Virgin Mary.*

The "General Introduction" makes clear that "in the womb of the Virgin of Nazareth, Jesus the Son of God took our human nature and became the Mediator of the Old and the New Covenant."[7] It continues, "Mary . . . 'was intimately involved in the history of salvation' [and] was actively present in various, wonderful ways in the mysteries of Christ's life."[8]

Thus, "Masses of the Blessed Virgin Mary have their meaning and purpose from her close participation in the history of salvation. Therefore when the Church commemorates the role of the Mother of the Lord in the work of redemption or honors her privileges, it is above all celebrating the events of salvation in which, by God's salvific plan, the Blessed Virgin was involved in view of the mystery of Christ."[9]

The "General Introduction" exhorts "priests and all others who have pastoral responsibilities . . . to teach the faithful that the eucharistic sacrifice is the memorial of the death and resurrection of Christ." They are "to point out the power of Mary's example that can do so much for the sanctification of the faithful."[10]

2) Mariology Is Grounded in Ecclesiology

Out of all of the documents of Vatican II, the placement of the only chapter which deals with Mary within the "Dogmatic Constitution of the Church" is itself enough to speak of the necessity that Mariology be grounded in ecclesiology. However, the fathers of the council declare that Mary "is the image and beginning of the Church as it is to be perfected in the world to come." She is "a sign of certain hope and comfort to the pilgrim People of God."[11]

In the Congregation for Divine Worship Decree in the *Collection of Masses of the Blessed Virgin Mary,* Cardinal Mayer and Archbishop Noe echo this teaching when they write of Mary: "She is revered by the Church as the New Eve, who, in view of the death of her Son, received at the moment of her conception a higher form of redemption."[12]

"She is revered as Mother, who through the power of the Holy Spirit gave virginal birth to her Son. She is revered as the disciple of Christ, who treasured in her heart the words of Christ the Master. She is revered as the faithful companion of the Redeemer, who, as God had planned, devoted herself with selfless generosity to her Son's mission."[13]

They continue: "The Church also sees in the Blessed Virgin a preeminent and unique member, graced with all virtue. The Church lovingly cherishes her and never ceases to ask for her protection, for she is the Mother entrusted to us by Christ on the altar of the cross."[14]

The "General Introduction" re-emphasizes the importance of ecclesiology as a Mariological foundation when it states that "the Church at the beginning of the liturgical year celebrates the work of God in preparing the Mother of the Redeemer."[15] Likewise, "the Church . . . celebrates God's intervention in human history in the celebration of the incarnation of the Word, the birth of Christ and its revelation to the shepherds and the magi, and in the celebration of other events of Christ's infancy. Mary was intimately involved in all of these saving deeds of God."[16]

"The Church's liturgical celebration of the public life of our Savior, which was marked by the glorious deeds of the Father, is also a commemoration of the Blessed Virgin,"[17] declares the "General Introduction." "The Church above all celebrates God's wonderful deeds in Christ's paschal mystery and in this celebration finds Mary intimately joined to her Son."[18]

The fathers of Vatican II stress this when they declare that "the Blessed Virgin's salutary influence on men originates not in any inner necessity but in the disposition of God. It flows forth from the superabundance of the merits of Christ, rests on his mediation, depends entirely on it and draws all its power from it."[19]

This is best exemplified in liturgical celebration, according to the "General Introduction": "Because of its bonds with Mary, the Church wishes 'to live the mystery of Christ' with her and like her and, above all in the liturgy, continually finds that the Blessed Virgin is ever present as the Mother of the Church and its advocate."[20] "Thus, in union with the Blessed Virgin and in imitation of her reverent devotion, the Church celebrates the divine mysteries by which 'God is perfectly glorified and the participants made holy.' "[21]

The fathers of the council declare, "By reason of the gift and role of her divine motherhood, by which she is united with her Son, the Redeemer, and with her unique graces and functions, the Blessed Virgin is also intimately united to the Church. . . . The mother of God is a type of the Church."[22]

The "General Introduction" states that Mary is an exemplar, a figure, and an image of the Christian life. "Particularly when the liturgy seeks to highlight her sanctity and to present her to the faithful as the devoted handmaid of the Father and the perfect disciple of Christ, the liturgy calls her the *exemplar*. It calls her a *figure* when it seeks to indicate that her manner of life as virgin, spouse, and mother provides a portrait of the life of the Church and shows the path it must take in its journey of faith and its following of Christ. Finally, the liturgy refers to her as *image*, in order to make it clear that in the Blessed Virgin, who is already perfectly fashioned in the likeness of her Son, the Church 'joyfully contemplates, as in a flawless image, that which the Church itself desires and hopes wholly to be.' "[23]

In summary, "Mary's example urges the faithful: to treasure the word of God in their hearts and dwell upon it assiduously; to praise God exultantly and thank him joyously; to serve God and neighbor faithfully and offer themselves generously; to pray with perseverance and make their petitions with confidence; to act in all things with mercy and humility; to cherish the law of God and embrace it with love; to love God in everything and above everything else; to be ready to meet Christ when he comes."[24] Indeed, "the celebration of the eucharist provides the faithful with an overview of the entire history of salvation and of the bonds that have joined Mary to the mystery of Christ and the Church."[25]

Mariology Is United with the Theology of the Communion of Saints

Even though Mary is "redeemed in a more exalted fashion by reason of the merits of her Son and united to him by a close and indissoluble tie," and, thus, she "far surpasses all creatures, both in heaven and on earth, . . . being of the race of Adam, she is at the same time also united to all those who are to be saved."[26]

Cardinal Mayer and Archbishop Noe declare, "The Church proclaims Mary as companion and sister in the journey of faith and in the adversities of life. In Mary, enthroned at Christ's side in the kingdom of heaven, the Church joyfully contemplates the image of its own future glory.''[27]

''By her maternal charity, she cares for the brethren of her Son, who still journey on earth surrounded by dangers and difficulties, until they are led into their blessed home. Therefore the Blessed Virgin is invoked in the Church under the titles of Advocate, Helper, Benefactress, and Mediatrix. This, however, is so understood that it neither takes away anything from nor adds anything to the dignity and efficacy of Christ the one Mediator.''[28]

Mary is a fellow member of the great communion of saints. If there is a social hierarchy in heaven, she has first place within it. ''She is hailed as preeminent and as a wholly unique member of the Church.''[29]

Notes

1. "Dogmatic Constitution on the Church" (hereafter DCC), November 21, 1964, *Vatican Council II: The Conciliar and Post Conciliar Documents,* Austin Flannery, ed., study edition (Northport, N.Y.: Costello Publishing Company, 1987) par. 54.
   2. Ibid.
   3. Ibid., par. 62.
   4. "General Introduction," *Collection of Masses of the Blessed Virgin Mary* (hereafter CMBVM) (Collegeville, Minn.: The Liturgical Press, 1992) par. 19.
   5. Ibid., par. 23.
   6. Ibid., p. 9.
   7. Ibid., par. 4.
   8. Ibid., par. 5.
   9. Ibid., par. 6.
   10. Ibid., par. 18.
   11. DCC, par. 68.
   12. CMBVM, p. 9.
   13. Ibid.
   14. Ibid.
   15. Ibid., par. 7.
   16. Ibid., par. 8.
   17. Ibid., par. 9.
   18. Ibid., par. 10.
   19. DCC, par. 60.

20. CMBVM, par. 12.
21. Ibid., par. 13.
22. DCC, par. 63.
23. CMBVM, par. 15.
24. Ibid., par. 17.
25. Ibid., par. 32.
26. DCC, par. 53.
27. CMBVM, p. 9.
28. DCC, par. 62.
29. Ibid., par. 53.

Chapter II

Marian Celebrations during the Liturgical Year

January 1

Solemnity of Mary, Mother of God

God's Smile

Scripture: The LORD bless you and keep you!
The LORD let his face shine upon you, and
be gracious to you!
The LORD look upon you kindly and give you peace!
(Num 6:24-26)

Mass: Num 6:22-27; Gal 4:4-7; Luke 2:16-21

Reflection: When a person blesses another, the one blessed is set aside as holy. God is called upon to watch over and to care for the blessed one. The person who is blessed is sacred. God smiles upon this person and offers him or her the gift of happiness.

Mary, the mother of God, is a blessed person. God chose Mary and set her apart from other people to be holy. He watched over her and cared for her. God's smile was the Holy Spirit, who overshadowed her and caused the new life of Jesus, God's only Son, to stir in her womb. This made her very happy.

God continues to bless people. Yes, all people have been set aside as holy or sacred by God. God smiles on a person when he or she is kept safe from the automobile accident that almost happened but didn't. After surgery when the tumor is discovered to be benign, a person may realize that God has kept him or her safe.

God's graciousness can be found in a clear, crisp winter's morning or in a bright, breezy spring day. The kindness of God can be found in the eyes of a couple who cradle in their arms their first child. On the face of the old the lines of God's years can easily be seen.

Blessings from God abound. None compares to the blessing of God's own Son which was given to Mary. She alone bears the title of the mother of God. Nevertheless, everyone has a share in God's blessings; God keeps smiling on people.

Meditation: What do you consider to be the three greatest blessings that you have received from God?

Prayer: Lord, once you chose a people and blessed them with your care. You kept them safe and showered upon them your graciousness. In time you chose Mary to be the mother of your only Son, our Lord Jesus Christ. You bestowed upon her your graciousness. Look upon us with similar kindness. Help us to know happiness in serving you. Give us the gift of your peace. We ask this through our Lord Jesus Christ, who lives and reigns with you and the Holy Spirit, one God, for ever and ever. Amen.

February 11

Optional Memorial of Our Lady of Lourdes
Nursing on Grace

Scripture: Rejoice with Jerusalem and be glad because of her,
all you who love her;
Exult, exult with her,
all you who were mourning over her!
Oh, that you may suck fully
of the milk of her comfort,

That you may nurse with delight
at her abundant breasts!

(Isa 66:10-11)

Mass: Isa 66:10-14; Common of the Blessed Virgin Mary

Reflection: One of the most moving sights is a mother breast-feeding her child. Some people consider it to be socially unacceptable for a woman to breast-feed her child in public, but, if carefully thought about, it is easily seen as one of the most human activities.

A man and a woman conceive a child. The woman, however, carries the child for nine months. She cares for it; she feeds it through her own body; she offers it the rhythm of her own heartbeat. Then, once the child is born, the mother continues to feed him or her with the milk of her own body. She continues to share her life with the life of her child. She has a special relationship with the child that the father will never know.

For a variety of reasons many women choose not to breast-feed their children. Instead a baby bottle with formula is used. There is absolutely nothing wrong with this approach, but it does pale in comparison to the scene of the mother holding the hungry, sucking child to her breasts and sharing her own life with her child.

The prophet Isaiah compared Jerusalem, the city where God lived, to a woman who had given birth to a child through suffering. The prophet's wish was that people would come to the holy city and find God's comfort, just as a child finds comfort when sucking at his or her mother's breasts. In fact, the prophet's wish was that all people might be filled with the joy that flowed from the abundance of the presence of God in Jerusalem.

Mary, the mother of Jesus, by accepting God's will for her, sucked fully of God's grace. She, in turn, offered her life in giving birth to Jesus, who nursed at her breasts. Jesus called and still calls all people to discern God's will and to draw comfort from God, his Father, the source of all life.

Meditation: Identify three ways in which you nurse on God's abundant breasts of grace.

Prayer: Lord, once you established your dwelling place in Jerusalem and invited all people to come and suck fully of your comfort. Now, through the birth of Jesus, your Son, you have come to live in the hearts of all who believe. Give us the faith of Mary, the mother of Jesus. Enable us to nurse on your grace and to share your life with others. We ask this through our Lord Jesus Christ, your Son, who lives and reigns with you and the Holy Spirit, one God, for ever and ever. Amen.

May 31

Feast of the Visitation

Hospitality

Scripture: Let love be sincere; hate what is evil, hold on to what is good; love one another with mutual affection; anticipate one another in showing honor. . . . Contribute to the needs of the holy ones, exercise hospitality (Rom 12:9, 13).

Mass: Zeph 3:14-18 or Rom 12:9-16; Luke 1:39-56

Reflection: Most guides for living a healthy life are based on what one should not do. A person should not become sedentary, eat foods high in fats and cholesterol, or fail to get an annual medical check-up. If these guides are followed, a person has a better chance of living a longer, healthier life.

While such practices take care of the individual, what about the way that people take care of each other? Oftentimes, sincerity is lacking when it comes to genuine care of another. This may not be done maliciously but because a person has so many things to take care of that he or she just institutionalizes others.

Genuine love for others springs from deep inside each person; it cannot be forced. When one person loves his or her community of believers, this person has come to understand the real meaning of love. He or she is genuinely concerned about others' needs. He or she honors the members of his or her religious family.

This is nothing other than hospitality. Mutual love welcomes others into one's inner circle, where security and honor are found. When one visits another and is welcomed hospitably, God is there.

As Luke portrays the scene, Mary visits Elizabeth, who welcomes her with honor, hospitality, and love. In the midst of this visit, God is there. Every time people create an environment of freedom in which everyone is received with genuine hospitality God is there.

Meditation: When did you last experience the genuine hospitality of another and discover the presence of God?

Prayer: God of love, you reveal your presence when your people welcome each other in genuine hospitality. Mary visited Elizabeth and was received with sincerity, love, and affection. Give us the spirit of genuine hospitality that we might always welcome others into our inner circle and know your presence in our lives. We ask this through our Lord Jesus Christ, your Son, who lives and reigns with you and the Holy Spirit, one God, for ever and ever. Amen.

Saturday following the Second Sunday after Pentecost

Optional Memorial of the Immaculate Heart of Mary

Heart

Scripture: [Jesus] went down with [his parents] and came to Nazareth, and was obedient to them; and his mother kept all these things in her heart (Luke 2:51).

Mass: Luke 2:41-51; Common of the Blessed Virgin Mary

Reflection: Something which is declared to be immaculate is spotlessly clean. Something immaculate has no flaw or blemish. When someone says, "This room is immaculate," he or she means that the room is very clean. To tell someone, "You look immaculate," is to declare that that person's clothes are neatly pressed and without wrinkle and that his or her appearance is in order—combed hair, manicured nails, trimmed beard, just the right amount of make-up.

The heart is that organ in the body which pumps blood throughout the circulatory system. However, the word "heart" often refers to the emotional center of a person. Love and hate, courage and fear, trust and hurt are located in the heart. A person who says, "Have a heart," is referring to human compassion. "Learn this by heart," means to memorize it. Although most of these functions take place in the brain, they are often stationed in the heart.

Mary, the mother of Jesus, pondered things in her heart. After the birth of Jesus and the visit of the shepherds, Mary treasured these events in her heart. Likewise, after finding Jesus in the temple, Mary thought about this event in her heart. In the pure heart of the mother of God were stored the wonders of God's revelation to his people.

God continues to reveal himself in people's hearts. This is often referred to as meditation. A person sits quietly, and, without saying a word, reflects on the events of the day. He or she searches for the presence of God in the early morning routine, in the on-the-job encounter, during the lunch break discussion, while driving home in the evening, at table with the family for supper, etc. In these events one discovers that God has been leading and guiding, helping one to grow in grace, helping one to understand the ways of God. By searching through these things, a person stores them in his or her heart

Meditation: What events from yesterday reveal God's activity in your life? How can you store these things in your heart?

Prayer: God of Jesus, in the Temple your Son taught the teachers, listening to them and asking them questions. He was about your business, revealing your presence in the human heart. Give us hearts like Mary, the mother of Jesus. With your Holy Spirit guide our daily reflection that we might recognize the many signs of your presence and store these things in our hearts. We ask this through our Lord Jesus Christ, who lives and reigns with you and the Holy Spirit, one God, for ever and ever. Amen.

July 16

Optional Memorial of Our Lady of Mount Carmel
Wisdom

Scripture: "The LORD begot me, the first-born of his ways,
    the forerunner of his prodigies of long ago;
From of old I was poured forth
    at the first, before the earth. . . .
Then was I beside him as his craftsman,
    and I was his delight day by day,
Playing before him all the while,
    playing on the surface of his earth. . . . "
(Prov 8:22-23, 30-31)

Mass: Prov 8:22-31; Common of the Blessed Virgin Mary

Reflection: God is said to be all-wise; that is, God is wisdom. God's wisdom can be personified, given the attributes of a person, so that invisible wisdom can be made visible, and thus understandable. Anthropomorphically, God's wisdom is what is named today common sense.

Common sense was what God first begot (of course, since there is no time with God, God had always begot common sense). The first great event was the birth of wisdom, who was born before the creation of the world.

Then, just as a child sits in his or her high chair and observes his or her parents, wisdom or common sense watched God create the heavens and the earth. Wisdom observed everything that was made.

But wisdom also was God's craftsman, the one who offered God the plan for the universe. Wisdom was God's architect, who drew the plans and prescribed the dimensions for the universe. Wisdom was the infinite mind of God, who, like a child, sat next to the Creator and played before him.

The wisdom of God became flesh in Jesus of Nazareth, who was born of Mary. God's eternal wisdom took on human flesh in

God's own Son. Common sense was objectified in Jesus. In him, God revealed the vastness of God's own wisdom.

This infinite vastness has not been exhausted. Mary's Son taught people how to honor the wise Creator. But more importantly, Jesus taught all people how to live a new life. It is the wisdom of this new life which continues to be revealed in every generation.

Meditation: In what area are you truly wise? In other words, of which of the ways of God are you capable of functioning as an architect and providing plans for others?

Prayer: God of wisdom, before the creation of the heavens and the earth, your eternal wisdom was guiding your hand and directing your thoughts. When time had run its course, your wisdom took flesh in the person of Jesus, born of Mary. He was your only-begotten Son, your delight. Through him you have made us your children. Fill us with your Spirit of wisdom that you might find delight day by day in us as we play before you. We ask this through our Lord Jesus Christ, who lives and reigns with you and the Holy Spirit, one God, for ever and ever. Amen.

August 5

Optional Memorial of the Dedication of St. Mary Major

Clothes

Scripture: I rejoice heartily in the LORD,
   in my God is the joy of my soul;
For he has clothed me with a robe of salvation,
   and wrapped me in a mantle of justice,
Like a bridegroom adorned with a diadem,
   like a bride bedecked with her jewels.

(Isa 61:10)

Mass: Isa 61:9-11; Common of the Blessed Virgin Mary

Reflection: Every morning people around the world arise from sleep, step into a warm shower, emerge from a new day's baptismal cleansing, and dress. One's dress might consist of pants, shirt, blouse, skirt, socks, etc. The clothes that a person wears not only protect one's body, but they function as a decoration for it. Also, clothes disclose something about the person who wears them.

It is no accident that a newly-baptized individual receives new clothes after baptism—usually a white garment. The person just baptized puts on Christ; that is, he or she is dressed in Christ through baptismal immersion—death and resurrection. The clothes signify that this individual has been formed in the image of Christ.

God chose to dress Mary in special clothes. Mary was clothed in a robe of salvation before the Savior was born. God baptized Mary before baptism was invented. God wrapped Mary in his protective mantle so that she would be the worthy mother of his own Son. Mary was formed into the image of Jesus, her only Son, before he was conceived in her womb.

God continues to offer special clothes to people. Today, God's gift is often referred to as grace. Through the suffering and death of Jesus, God has made it possible for all people to be wrapped in his robe of salvation. The day of baptism signifies the beginning of this process, which lasts throughout a person's lifetime.

A person who is wrapped in God's clothes is chosen and protected by God. Such a person discloses the great things that God continues to do in the world.

Meditation: Identify three ways in which your clothes disclose God's activity in your life.

Prayer: Lord God, you never cease to call people to new life through the waters of baptism. You clothe us in your robe of salvation and you wrap us in your mantle of justice. Just as you adorned Mary, the mother of your Son, bedeck us with your grace. May we, like her, always rejoice heartily in you, the joy of our souls. We ask this through our Lord Jesus Christ, your Son, who lives and reigns with you and the Holy Spirit, one God, for ever and ever. Amen.

August 15

Solemnity of the Assumption of Mary
Vigil Mass: Incorruptible and Immortal

Scripture: When this which is corruptible clothes itself with incorruptibility and this which is mortal clothes itself with immortality, then the word that is written shall come about:

> "Death is swallowed up in victory.
> Where, O death, is your victory?
> Where, O death, is your sting?"
> (1 Cor 15:54-55)

Mass: 1 Chr 15:3-4, 15, 16; 16:1-2; 1 Cor 15:54-57; Luke 11:27-28

Reflection: The Solemnity of the Assumption of Mary is a celebration of her resurrection. Since she was the mother of Jesus, God's only Son, and since she was preserved from the stain of sin, she, like Jesus, was raised by God to the joys of eternal life. Mary was the first, after Christ, to experience resurrection.

All people are corruptible; that is, every person is made of flesh and blood, which die. Once a dead person is buried, he or she decomposes. After a few years, there is little left to indicate that such a person ever walked on the face of the earth.

All people are mortal; that is, every person will die some day. No one lives for ever. Modern medicine and technology may be able to preserve life for eighty, ninety, or one hundred years, but sooner or later the fate of every human being is to die. Death is an event which no one can escape.

Through the resurrection of Jesus, however, God has turned what is corruptible and mortal into the incorruptible and the immortal. When God raised Jesus from the dead and bestowed new and eternal life upon him, he also made it possible for every human being to be raised from the dead and to share in this new and eternal life. The human body will still die and decompose, but God has demonstrated that this is not the end.

God defeated death by raising Jesus from the dead. He clothed the risen body of Jesus in incorruptibility and immortality. Death lost the battle; God took the victory. After Jesus, Mary was the first to be raised from the dead and to be dressed in God's incorruptible and immortal life. What God did for Jesus and Mary will be done for every person of faith.

Meditation: Daily, how do you experience corruptibility and mortality? How can these experiences lead you to hope for incorruptibility and immortality?

Prayer: Incorruptible and immortal God, by raising Jesus from the dead you conquered the power of death and won the victory of new and eternal life. Because of her faithfulness, you raised Mary from the dead so that she might immediately share in your Son's incorruptible and immortal life. When we are overcome with corruptibility and mortality, give us the hope that one day we may be counted worthy to be raised to the new life you share with Jesus and the Holy Spirit, one God, for ever and ever. Amen.

August 15

Solemnity of the Assumption of Mary
Mass during the Day: Harvest

Scripture: Now Christ has been raised from the dead, the first-fruits of those who have fallen asleep. For since death came through a human being, the resurrection of the dead came also through a human being (1 Cor 15:20-21).

Mass: Rev 11:19; 12:1-6, 10; 1 Cor 15:20-26; Luke 1:39-56

Reflection: The firstfruits were the initial results of the vineyards and fields. The firstfruits in Old Testament times were brought to God in the Temple as signs of thanksgiving for the produce of the land. By offering the firstfruits, people dedicated the whole harvest to God, who had made the tree blossom and the seed grow.

The resurrection of Jesus is a firstfruit. It is the initial result of one human being who did God's will. The fullness of the harvest is yet to come. This means that there are more people who, following the example of Jesus, can do God's will and be raised from the dead. The raising of Jesus is but a prelude to the raising of everyone in the great harvest at the end of time.

Mary, the mother of Jesus, has already followed Jesus. Because of her special place in the plan of salvation, she was preserved from sin. God chose to raise her from the dead, so that she already has been harvested and shares in eternal life. For Mary, just as for Jesus, God has destroyed death.

Today, those who follow Christ faithfully find in Jesus and in Mary their hope for the harvest at the end of time. Just as God raised his own Son from the dead, and then the mother of his Son, he promises that he will raise every human being from the dead. Christ's resurrection and Mary's assumption are held out as validations of God's promise.

It is important to note that the harvest is a corporate event. The whole human race was at one time subject to death because of one human being's disobedience. But through another human being's obedience, the whole human race can now share in the resurrection. Christ is the firstfruits of the resurrection-harvest. Because of her unique and singular place, Mary is the second to be raised from the dead. The complete harvest is yet to come.

Meditation: In what ways do you experience the new life of the resurrection? In what ways is Mary a sign of hope for you?

Prayer: God of the harvest, once death came through a human being whom you created; in Adam all people died. However, through the obedience of Jesus, your Son, you gave us the gift of the resurrection of the dead. Now, in Christ, the firstfruits of your harvest, all people can be brought to life. Trace in us the lines of Mary's obedience to your word. Form us into the image of Jesus, that we might be raised to the eternal life he shares with you and the Holy Spirit, one God, for ever and ever. Amen.

August 22

Memorial of the Queenship of Mary
Darkness to Light

Scripture: The people who walked in darkness
have seen a great light;
Upon those who dwelt in the land of gloom
a light has shone. . . .
For a child is born to us, a son is given us;
upon his shoulder dominion rests.
They name him Wonder-Counselor, God-Hero,
Father-Forever, Prince of Peace.

(Isa 9:1, 5)

Mass: Isa 9:1-6; Luke 1:39-47

Reflection: When people are oppressed, they are in darkness. When one country is occupied by another, a whole nation is in darkness. The despair of one individual is a type of darkness. Any-time a people, a nation, or a person is in darkness, light or deliverance is sought. Oppression, occupation, and despair breed a strong hope for a day of light.

When people walk in darkness, they usually conclude that God has abandoned them. They are, of course, wrong. Usually, it is the people who have abandoned God. When the people repent, they begin to find their way once again; they can walk in the light.

Sometimes this hope for light crystallizes in a child. The birth of a child can make hope incarnate, give it flesh. For the people of northern Palestine, the Assyrian invasion was darkness and gloom, but Isaiah's declaration that a child would be born with authority gave them hope.

This child, originally a reference to a future king, would possess a remarkable wisdom and prudence. He would be a warrior, who would be looked upon as a hero by his people because he would defend them and always be devoted to them. With his power he would establish peace. Thus, darkness would be turned into light.

Christianity has interpreted this hoped-for child as Jesus of Nazareth, Mary's Son. Because Mary gave birth, made hope incarnate, she is honored as the queen of heaven, who sits near the throne of her Son, Christ the King.

Jesus was not a warrior or a hero. However, through his parables he taught wisdom. He was devoted to people. He called for a peace that the world cannot give. This was not the type of kingship for which people had hoped, but it did turn darkness into light.

Meditation: How does God continue to turn your darkness into light? Identify three recent darknesses which have been transformed into light by God.

Prayer: God of light, when your people walked in darkness, you sent them the great light, Jesus, who was born of Mary. As your only-begotten Son, he taught us wisdom and prudence, peace and justice. As king of heaven and earth, he reigned from the cross, and he made Mary the queen of your people. When we are overcome with darkness, give us the light of Jesus, your Son, who lives and reigns with you and the Holy Spirit, one God, for ever and ever. Amen.

September 8

Feast of the Birth of Mary

"Nowheresville"

Scripture: You, Bethlehem-Ephrathah,
          too small to be among the clans of Judah,
      From you shall come forth for me
          one who is to be ruler in Israel;
      Whose origin is from of old,
          from ancient times.

(Mic 5:1)

Mass: Mic 5:1-4 or Rom 8:28-30; Matt 1:1-16, 18-23

Reflection: If one drives along back roads and stays off of the interstate highways, one will pass through many small towns. Sometimes, these towns consist of only a few buildings and a few hundred people. Many people say that they would never want to live in such places because they are so far away from the activity and possibilities of life in a city. Such small towns are often referred to as "Nowheresville."

Bethlehem-Ephrathah was a small town; that is, Bethlehem-Ephrathah was a "Nowheresville." In order to be sure that his readers would know what town he was talking about, the prophet Micah had to use both the old name for the town—Ephrathah—and the most recent name for it—Bethlehem. Bethlehem-Ephrathah was so small that the entering and leaving sign could have been placed on the same pole!

But what this town did have going for it was that it was the birthplace of David, the most powerful king of Israel. The promise made to David that his kingdom would never end is what gave Israel hope in the midst of enemy oppression and occupation. David was the messiah, the anointed of the Lord. The people hoped for a new messiah from David's line.

In time, Mary gave birth to Jesus, the hoped-for Messiah, the anointed of the Lord. In celebrating the birth of Mary, people remember the purpose of her birth: that she might conceive and bring forth the Messiah. Just as no one would have thought to look for God in Bethlehem-Ephrathah, "Nowheresville," so no one would have thought to look for God's Son in the womb of a maiden from Nazareth.

But this is exactly the point: God is not always found where God is expected to be; God is found where God chooses to live: "Nowheresville" and in maiden wombs!

Meditation: Where have you found God but did not expect to find God?

Prayer: God of David, you sent Samuel to Bethlehem-Ephrathah to anoint David, son of Jesse, to be the new king of Israel. David governed your people wisely and made of them a great nation. When your people were oppressed, you sent them Jesus, your anointed One, your only Son, who was born of Mary. He taught your people your way and reigned as king from a cross. Guide us in following our King and keep us loyal to him, who lives and reigns with you and the Holy Spirit, one God, for ever and ever. Amen.

September 15

Memorial of Our Lady of Sorrows

Obedience

Scripture: Son though he was, he learned obedience from what he suffered (Heb 5:8).

Mass: Heb 5:7-9; John 19:25-27 or Luke 2:33-35

Reflection: Today, few people like to hear the word "obedience," especially in the sense of submission to a higher authority. "Do what I tell you," a parent may tell a child. "Why can't you obey your teacher?" the principal may ask a student who has been sent to his or her office. After pulling over a car to the side of the road, the highway patrolman asks the driver, "Did you know that you were not obeying the speed limit?"

To be submissive to the command of another person is hard enough in a day of personal freedom, religious independence, and psychological individuality. It becomes even harder to predicate obedience of Jesus, the Son of God. But obedient he was.

Jesus was obedient to God's will, all the way to the cross. Because of his humanity—an aspect that is easily forgotten—Jesus suffered, like all people do. He knew loneliness, despair, thirst, hunger, betrayal of friends, etc. Through his human suffering he learned obedience to God's will. It was his obedience that made him perfect.

Mary, the mother of Jesus, another human being, knew suffering. She was filled with sorrow early in life. An unwed, pregnant teen-age girl cannot be devoid of suffering. She knew the suffering of childbirth, despair, resignation, and death. But like her Son, Mary learned obedience to God's word through her suffering. To call her "Our Lady of Sorrows" is to bestow a title upon her which declares that she is able to sympathize with human suffering.

While obedience carries negative connotations in the everyday world, it deserves positive reflection. If the Son of God was obedient to his Father, and if Mary, the mother of God, was obedient to the Father, then how can people today not learn obedience through suffering?

Meditation: How have you learned obedience to God's word through suffering?

Prayer: God of suffering, you did not remove the agony of your Son as he hung dying on the cross. Neither did you take away the suffering of his mother throughout her life. By drinking deeply of suffering both Jesus and Mary learned to be obedient to your word. Teach us this same obedience through suffering. Help us to know your will, to embrace it, and to do it in our lives. We ask this through our Lord Jesus Christ, who lives and reigns with you and the Holy Spirit, one God, for ever and ever. Amen.

October 7

Memorial of Our Lady of the Rosary
Overshadowed

Scripture: "The holy Spirit will come upon you, and the power of the Most High will overshadow you. Therefore the child to be born will be called holy, the Son of God" (Luke 1:35).

Mass: Luke 1:26-38; Common of the Blessed Virgin Mary

Reflection: Mary was a human being who was favored by God. She was graced by God. She was chosen by God to be the mother of God's only Son, Jesus.

The child she bore in her womb was conceived by the Holy Spirit. Like the pillar of cloud, a sign of God's presence, which accompanied the Israelites during the exodus from Egypt, God overshadowed Mary with his Spirit. Her child was the Son of God.

Today, however, God continues to cast his shadow, his Holy Spirit, upon people. While people do not conceive in the same way that Mary did, they nevertheless do bring forth new life through the Spirit at work in their lives.

A person who struggles with a moral decision, such as whether or not to remove a life-support system from an aged parent, prays for guidance. God overshadows this person with counsel from family, doctors, and nurses. The final decision, which brings peace, is the one conceived by the power of the Holy Spirit.

The Holy Spirit is active in the lives of a married couple. As they struggle through marriage, they seek help. Through prayer, God often sends another person into their lives. This other may say but a single word which supports their marriage. That single word is conceived by the Holy Spirit and received by the couple as an answer to their prayers.

Every time people ask God for help or guidance, God readily sends the Spirit. The Spirit is like a breath of fresh air, a moment of insight, a word of encouragement. The Spirit overshadows people and causes God's life to well up from deep within them.

Meditation: When did you most recently experience the overshadowing of the Holy Spirit?

Prayer: Most High God, you overshadowed Mary with the Holy Spirit and she conceived your only-begotten Son, our Lord Jesus Christ. Send the Holy Spirit into our lives. When we face moral dilemmas, send the Spirit as a guide. When we encounter marital problems, send the Spirit as a counselor. When doubts arise, send the Spirit as a friend. Overshadow us that we may conceive of your will and bring it to birth in our lives. We ask this through our Lord Jesus Christ, who lives and reigns with you and the Holy Spirit, one God, for ever and ever. Amen.

November 21

Memorial of the Presentation of Mary
Women

Scripture: The book of the genealogy of Jesus Christ, the son of David, the son of Abraham. Abraham became the father of Isaac, Isaac the father of Jacob, Jacob the father of Judah and his brothers. Judah became the father of Perez and Zerah, whose mother was Tamar, . . . Salmon the father of Boaz, whose mother was Rahab. Boaz became the father of Obed, whose mother was Ruth. Obed became the father of Jesse, Jesse the father of David the king. David became the father of Solomon, whose mother had been the wife of Uriah, . . . Jacob the father of Joseph, the husband of Mary (Matt 1:1-3, 5-6, 16).

Mass: Matt 1:1-16, 18-23; Common of the Blessed Virgin Mary

Reflection: In the Matthean genealogy of Jesus, the names of five women are mentioned. This fact would not be of particular importance except that these five women appear in an all-male genealogical list of names: Tamar, Rahab, Ruth, the wife of Uriah (Bathsheba), and Mary. The question, then, is why did the author include these women in his genealogy?

Tamar, Judah's daughter-in-law, dressed like a harlot and seduced her father-in-law. Through their union, she conceived and bore twins.

Rahab was the manager of a brothel in Jericho. When Joshua sent spies to reconnoiter the land, Rahab hid them from the king of Jericho.

Ruth was the mother of Obed, whose father was Boaz. After dressing in her finest robes, she placed herself at Boaz' feet in order to convince him to marry her and raise up heirs to her dead husband's name. Obed, her son, became the grandfather of David.

The wife of Uriah was Bathsheba; David saw her bathing on the roof, desired her, and conceived a child with her. Later, in order to cover up his sin, David sent Uriah into the front line of battle, where he was slain. David's and Bathsheba's child was born and died, but Bathsheba conceived again and gave birth to Solomon.

These four women bore sons through irregular and unexpected situations. However, even though their reputations are somewhat colored, they are remembered for doing God's will. In the Matthean understanding, they prepare the way for the supreme irregularity of birth, Jesus, the Son of God.

Mary, a virgin, is found to be with child through the Holy Spirit before she and Joseph live together. According to the Law, Joseph should expose her and see that she be stoned to death. But he does not follow the Law; according to divine intervention he takes her to be his wife and he claims the child as his own. Thus, the irregular birth of the Messiah, foreshadowed in the other four women, is brought about by God. God works God's will even in the lives of those people most would least expect.

Meditation: How has God been able to work his will through some irregularity in your life? in your family?

Prayer: God of Abraham and David, you accomplished your will in Tamar, Rahab, Ruth, and Bathsheba and brought forth the ancestors of your Son, Jesus Christ. Of Mary, the betrothed of Joseph, was born the Messiah. When our lives seem irregular and do not follow our pre-ordained plans, help us to see the possibility of your activity in our lives. Through your Holy Spirit create in us a desire to know your will and a longing to do it. We ask this through our Lord Jesus Christ, who lives and reigns with you and the Holy Spirit, one God, for ever and ever. Amen.

December 8

Solemnity of the Immaculate Conception
Chosen

Scripture: In him we were also chosen, destined in accord with the purpose of the One who accomplishes all things according to the intention of his will, so that we might exist for the praise of his glory, we who first hoped in Christ (Eph 1:11-12).

Mass: Gen 3:9-15, 20; Eph 1:3-6, 11-12; Luke 1:26-38

Reflection: Mary was chosen by God to be the mother of Jesus. From the moment that she was conceived in her mother's womb, God had picked Mary for his own special purpose. He preserved her from sin so that she might conceive the Christ in her womb. Mary's immaculate conception was a one-time-only event, but God's choosing of people continues today.

God wills that all people respond to his love. This was God's motivation for choosing Mary and for sending his own Son. God did not take away the freedom to say "No" to his love, but he demonstrated in Mary and Jesus his desire that everyone say "Yes."

God loves people so much that he wants them to be with him. The author of the Letter to the Ephesians declares this to be part of God's plan before the foundation of the world. Mary shared in this plan through the special privilege of being wrapped in God's grace. She was prepared by God to be a fitting mother for God-made-man.

Jesus, Mary's Son, was God's way of furthering his plan of adoption. Through Christ, all people are now heirs to God's grace, God's very self. This saving grace is undeserved; it is God's free gift out of his love.

All that people can do is accept the gift of grace and praise God for this free gift. In other words, all that people can do is respond, like Mary, to God's offer.

Meditation: Identify three ways that you have responded to God's offer of grace in the past month.

Prayer: Blessed are you, God and Father of our Lord Jesus Christ, for you have blessed us in Christ with every spiritual blessing. You chose us in Christ before the foundation of the world to be holy and without blemish before you. Just as you once wrapped Mary in your love, so clothe us with strength to respond to your will. Just as you once destined her to be the mother of your Christ, so implant in us your word with power to praise your glory. We ask this through our Lord Jesus Christ, your Son, who lives and reigns with you and the Holy Spirit, one God, for ever and ever. Amen.

December 12

Feast of Our Lady of Guadalupe
Presence

Scripture: God's temple in heaven was opened, and the ark of his covenant could be seen in the temple. . . . A great sign appeared in the sky, a woman clothed with the sun, with the moon under her feet, and on her head a crown of twelve stars (Rev 11:19–12:1).

Mass: Zech 2:14-17; Rev 11:19, 12:1-6, 10; Luke 1:39-47

Reflection: In the days of Solomon, king of Israel, a temple was built in Jerusalem for God. The ark, the box containing the tablets of the Law, Moses' staff, and a jar of manna, was placed in the Holy of Holies of the Temple. Above the ark cherubim held aloft their wings, which formed a throne for God. Thus, in a sense, the ark "contained" God.

Mary can be compared to the ark. Just as God chose to live in a temple made of wood and stone, so God came to live in the womb of Mary. The incarnation, the enfleshment of God—Jesus—took place in Mary's womb. Thus, like the ark of old, she "contained" God.

The author of the Book of Revelation employs Old Testament symbols to elucidate New Testament truths. Just as Joseph, twelfth son of Jacob, had a dream in which the sun and the moon and eleven stars bowed down to him, so too does the author of Revelation have a vision of a woman clothed with the sun, with the moon under her feet, and a crown of twelve stars on her head.

For Joseph the dream meant that his father, mother, and eleven brothers would bow down to him. One day Joseph would save his family from famine. He would offer them what they needed to live. As second-in-command in Egypt, he would have at his hand whatever was needed to sustain life.

For the author of the Book of Revelation, the sign in the sky represents God's people, who gave birth to the Messiah, as well as the new Israel, who followed the Messiah. The sun and moon do not bow down, as they do in Joseph's dream. Now they form the raiment of those who accept the Messiah. The eleven stars have become twelve, signifying the twelve tribes of Israel and the twelve apostles of the Lamb.

Just as God's presence in the sign of the ark gave birth to a nation, so too does Mary, the new ark, give birth to Jesus, the Son of God, who called people to a new way of life. Like Joseph who was able to offer sustenance to his family, Jesus offers himself for all people. Jesus promises eternal life.

Today, the Church is often referred to as a "mother," a woman about to give birth. The baptismal font is the womb of the Church, the source of new life. Every time that a person is baptized, born again, God's people increase. A new ark of God's presence is revealed to God's people.

Meditation: In what ways are you an ark of God's presence?

Prayer: God of heaven and earth, once you built your dwelling place in Jerusalem and made the ark in the Temple a sign of your presence. Then, you chose the virgin of Nazareth to be the mother of your Son, the incarnate sign of your love for all people. Through the waters of rebirth you make us into living temples of your Spirit. Make us signs of your presence. Clothe us with the light of your love. Enable us to be worthy of the crown of eternal life. We ask this through our Lord Jesus Christ, your Son, who lives and reigns with you and the Holy Spirit, one God, for ever and ever. Amen.

Chapter III

Collection of Masses
of the Blessed Virgin Mary

Advent Season

1. The Blessed Virgin Mary,
Chosen Daughter of Israel
Faith and Obedience

Scripture: The LORD said to Abram: "Go forth from the land of your kinsfolk and from your father's house to a land that I will show you." . . . Abram went as the LORD directed him (Gen 12:1, 4).

Mass: Gen 12:1-7 or 2 Sam 7:1-5, 8-11, 16; Matt 1:1-17

Reflection: Abram, later to be called Abraham, the father of Israel, is remembered for his faith and his obedience to God's word. When instructed by God to migrate from his own land and his own people, Abram obeyed; he believed that God's promise to make of him a great nation was worthy of his trust.

In a similar way, Mary, a descendant of Abram, is remembered for her faith and her obedience to God's word. When she was instructed by God that she was to bear a child, even though she was not yet married to Joseph, she obeyed; she believed that God's promise to her was worthy of her trust. Thus, Mary became the chosen daughter of Israel.

Jesus, Mary's Son, also demonstrated faith and obedience, even though he is the Son of God. Jesus of Nazareth placed his trust in his Father. He did his Father's will, which meant suffering and death on the cross. But throughout his life he believed that God was trustworthy. God demonstrated his trustworthiness by raising Jesus from the dead.

Faith and obedience to God's word are qualities for which God still looks in people today. God is particularly interested in people who are willing to pledge blind trust, to say that they believe no matter what crisis they face. God wants people of unquestioning faith.

Also, God wants people who will listen to and obey his word. Certainly, God has demonstrated how reliable he is in Abram, Mary, and Jesus. If God says "Go forth," people should be willing to travel unquestioning. If God says "Give birth," people should be willing unquestioning to bring forth new life. If God says "Sacrifice your life," people should be willing without doubt to give up their lives.

Meditation: How does your faith and your obedience to God's word compare to Abram's, Mary's, and Jesus'?

Prayer: God of Abraham, once you called your servant to leave his own land and his own people and to travel to a new land. He trusted in your promise, and you made of him a great nation. Mary, the mother of your only-begotten Son, heard your word and trusted in your promise. Give us attentive ears that we might hear your word in the events of our day. Give us the courage to say "Yes" and to obey your will. We ask this through our Lord Jesus Christ, your Son, who lives and reigns with you and the Holy Spirit, one God, for ever and ever. Amen.

2. The Blessed Virgin Mary and the Annunciation of the Lord
Promise Kept

Scripture: The virgin shall be with child, and bear a son, and shall name him Immanuel (Isa 7:14).

Mass: Isa 7:10-14; 8:10; Luke 1:26-38

Reflection: Frequently, a person receives announcements in the mail. Such announcements concern baby showers, wedding showers, births, marriages, and deaths. Sometimes the announcement is an invitation to attend an event, such as a birthday party. Other times, the announcement is a sharing of information.

When Israel was oppressed, the prophet Isaiah made an announcement to King Ahaz that God would fulfill his earlier promise to David and raise up a new king, who would restore the nation to its former Davidic grandeur. In other words, Isaiah offered the people hope in the midst of a hopeless situation. A child would be born; he would be the Messiah, the anointed of the Lord, the king of Israel, the hoped-for deliverer, the heir that God promised to David.

The name that this child would bear is Immanuel (or Emmanuel), which means "With us is God!" The child, according to Isaiah, would be the living sign of God's presence with his people, the living sign of God's fulfillment of his promise to David, the living sign of God's deliverance of his people.

Such a Messiah did not appear, however. In the course of time, the royal line of Israel's kings disappeared. Foreign powers conquered Israel and established their own form of government to prohibit any type of rebellion. But the promise of a Messiah, a descendant of David and the tribe of Judah, lived on in the hopes of the people.

The Church has always seen Isaiah's prophecy fulfilled in the birth of Jesus. God kept his promise to David by raising up the Nazarene from the tribe of Judah. Jesus was born of the Virgin Mary and anointed with God's Holy Spirit. He was not the warrior-king for whom people had hoped. His kingdom was not of this world.

He was, however, Immanuel, "With us is God." The announcement made to Mary (in Luke's Gospel) and to Joseph (in Matthew's Gospel) is that Jesus is the enfleshment of God. God could get no closer to the human race than by becoming a human being. Jesus is more than Isaiah's prophecy; he is God in the midst of people. Jesus, born of Mary, is the enfleshed promise of God, which has been kept.

Meditation: Recently, what announcement have you received from God?

Prayer: God of David and Isaiah, you promised your servant David that you would be with him and his heirs forever. In a time of distress, Isaiah reminded your people Israel of your faithfulness. From the tribe of Judah you raised up Jesus, born of the Virgin Mary, and anointed with your Holy Spirit; he proclaimed your kingdom and enfleshed your promise. When we despair, open our ears that we may hear the announcements that you make to us. Keep us faithful to your word and enable us to do your will. We ask this through our Lord Jesus Christ, your Son and Immanuel, who lives and reigns with you and the Holy Spirit, one God, for ever and ever. Amen.

3. The Visitation of the Blessed Virgin Mary
Visits

Scripture: Shout for joy, O daughter Zion!
  sing joyfully, O Israel!
Be glad and exult with all your heart,
  O daughter Jerusalem!
The King of Israel, the LORD, is in your midst,
  you have no further misfortune to fear.
  (Zeph 3:14, 15)

Mass: Zeph 3:14-18 or Song 2:8-14; Luke 1:39-56

Reflection: When people spend time together, they visit with each other. A visit can consist of either a few minutes or a few days spent sharing words, food, and, consequently, life with another person or with several other people.

Sometimes people travel great distances to visit with others; sometimes they travel down the street. Families spend a whole day visiting with each other on Thanksgiving, Easter, and Christmas. During the summer, a family reunion is nothing other than a great visiting session. Even at work, during break times or lunch, co-workers visit with each other. Letter writing is also a type of visiting.

The desire to visit is a human need. People want to share their lives with other people. They may begin with the weather, which is a way of sharing something that everyone experiences and understands, but eventually they get to the nitty-gritty of life—birth, suffering, celebration, and death.

The birth of child to a member of the family is a cause of joy. The immediate members of the family tell the whole world about it. Mothers share the labor pains. Fathers share their pride. Siblings talk about the "new addition." Grandparents are pleased to add "grand" before their titles.

Suffering is spoken about among the mature members of the family. "Remember Uncle John?" one asks. "He died of cancer ten years ago." Yes, he is still remembered, but so is his suffering. "Aunt Ann lived a hard life," someone else says. The conversation continues to share suffering.

Birthday visits are times of celebration. New life is remembered as the years pass by. The good experiences of older lives are recalled. People sing and make merry. They remember the "good old days," and they face the future with hope.

Visiting also includes a few words about death. The inevitability of death cannot be avoided, as it touches everyone sooner or later. When one person can hold another and understand the pain of death, a visit has taken place. No words need to be exchanged. A hug, a kiss, a pat on the back, a shoulder upon which to shed a tear can help to know the truth and finality of death.

Just as people visit with each other, so too does God visit with people. The yearning that people have to be with each other is also found in God's desire to be with people. In fact, God is always in the midst of people. God is present everywhere and always. People may not be aware of this presence, but God is there.

Mary, the mother of Jesus, knew God's presence in a special way. She was visited by God and asked to be the mother of God's only-begotten Son. She conceived this child by the power of the Holy Spirit; thus, God was not only in her midst, but God took up residence in flesh in her womb. Mary was the chosen daughter of Israel.

Meditation: In which three recent events has God visited with you?

Prayer: King of Israel, Lord God, because you are always in our midst, we have nothing to fear. Through births, sufferings, celebrations, and death, you visit us. Once you chose your daughter, Mary, to be the mother of your Son, our Lord Jesus Christ. You overshadowed her with the power of your Holy Spirit. Send that same Spirit to us that we might know your constant presence in our lives. Then, we can shout and sing for joy in praise of you, Father, Son, and Holy Spirit, one God, for ever and ever. Amen.

Christmas Season

4. Holy Mary, Mother of God
Adoption

Scripture: When the fullness of time had come, God sent his Son, born of a woman, born under the law, to ransom those under the law, so that we might receive adoption (Gal 4:4-5).

Mass: Gal 4:4-7; Luke 2:15-19

Reflection: Parents who adopt a child take the boy or girl by choice; freely, they choose to enter into a parent-child relationship. This parent-child relationship will, hopefully, benefit both parents and child. Voluntarily, parents accept an adopted child as their own.

God, like a parent, has adopted every person. God has chosen to enter into a relationship with every human being. This God-human relationship benefits both God and people. Voluntarily, God accepts people as his own when he adopts them.

The agency for adoption which God chose was the incarnation. An intense interest in people led God to send his only-begotten Son as a man. By becoming flesh, Jesus, the Son of God, made it possible for every human person to become an adopted son or daughter of God.

Jesus was born under the Law; that is, he was a Jew, subject to the laws of the covenant, which were given to Moses. He was fully human, demonstrated in his birth from a woman, Mary.

In the fullness of time, God chose Mary to be the mother of Jesus, who was God. Therefore, Mary is rightly called the mother of God. God adopted her as his daughter through the incarnation of the Son.

Today, God continues to adopt people. Through the waters of baptism, every person is delivered from an old way of life and called to a new status, an adopted child of God and an heir of God's kingdom.

Meditation: In which ways does your adoptive relationship with God benefit you? In which ways does it benefit God?

Prayer: Father, when the fullness of time had come, you sent your own Son, born of Mary, born under the Law, to ransom us from the Law. Through his birth and suffering and death, you made us your adopted sons and daughters. We have been immersed into his paschal mystery through the waters of baptism. Keep us faithful to our baptismal promises that we might become heirs of the kingdom, where you live and reign with Jesus and the Holy Spirit, one God, for ever and ever. Amen.

5. The Blessed Virgin Mary, Mother of the Savior
Motherhood

Scripture: The time came for her to have her child, and she gave birth to her firstborn son. She wrapped him in swaddling clothes and laid him in a manger (Luke 2:6-7).

Mass: Isa 9:1-3, 5-6; Luke 2:1-14

Reflection: Every human being has a mother, the woman who brought him or her to life. For every person in the world there is a woman who is responsible for his or her birth. One may have been abandoned or given up for adoption by one's mother, but, nevertheless, one has a physical mother.

Motherhood can be expanded to include those who function as mothers. In the case of an adopted child, the adoptive woman cares for the child as her own and becomes the child's mother. She may not have given birth physically to the child, but she shares the joys and sorrows of a mother.

Sometimes, others fulfill the role of mother. A grandparent may nurture a child. An aunt may take a special interest in a child. A woman who is not related by blood may raise a child. In all of these cases, the woman assumes the role of mother.

The Son of God was born of a mother. Jesus was nourished at the breasts of Mary. He was cared for by the Virgin of Nazareth. Mary's motherhood is focused on her child—Jesus, the Son of God.

In Mary one can also see the motherhood of God. Since God is neither male nor female, God is both father and mother. With a father's love, God overshadowed Mary and she conceived God's Son through the power of the Holy Spirit. With a mother's love, God watched over this chosen daughter, as she gave birth to her firstborn son. Mary's motherhood reveals the beauty of the motherhood of God.

Meditation: In what ways is God your mother?

Prayer: God, our mother, you bring about our conception in the depths of our mother's wombs. At the appropriate time, you bring us to birth and lavish a mother's love upon us. You feed us with the milk of your word and enable us to suck with comfort at the breasts of the sacraments of your Church. Make of us gentle mothers, like Mary, the mother of Jesus. May we always be willing to reveal your tender love to the world. We ask this through our Lord Jesus Christ, your Son, who lives and reigns with you and the Holy Spirit, one God, for ever and ever. Amen.

6. The Blessed Virgin Mary and the Epiphany of the Lord
Light

Scripture: Rise up in splendor! Your light has come,
the glory of the LORD shines upon you.
See, darkness covers the earth,
and thick clouds cover the peoples;

But upon you the LORD shines,
and over you appears his glory.

(Isa 60:1-2)

Mass: Isa 60:1-6; Matt 2:1-12

Reflection: As the procession with the Easter candle makes its way into the church during the Easter Vigil, the deacon sings, "Christ our light." The candle's flame, taken from the new fire kindled outside of the church, represents the new life of the resurrection. God raised Jesus from the dead and made him as radiant as light.

Mary, the mother of Jesus, was the first to experience God's light when she conceived Jesus in the darkness of her womb. When she accepted her mission to be the mother of God, her light had come; the glory of God shined upon her. As she was wrapped in God's light from the moment of the incarnation, she also shared in its fullness when God raised her from the dead and shared with her the light of her Son's resurrection.

Mary brought the light to a world covered with darkness. People felt like they were trapped in a fog; they could not see where they were going. Like a bright light on a foggy night, Jesus taught people a new way of life and light. By facing the darkness of death, Jesus demonstrated the light of the resurrection.

The light of Jesus continues to be spread through the darkness of the world today. Every time someone returns a kind word for something said in anger or hatred, light dispels darkness. When a parent chooses to teach a child the right way instead of to yell and scream at him or her, darkness flees before the light of knowledge. If one person tells the whole truth to another, even though much pain may be involved, the light shines and darkness is overcome.

The light of the child that Mary conceived and brought forth continues to shine whenever followers of Jesus choose to be light instead of darkness. This is how God continues to make his glory appear.

Meditation: In the past three days, in what ways have you been light instead of darkness? In what ways have you been darkness instead of light?

Prayer: God of light, your glory shines upon us. Through the birth of your Son, Jesus, the darkness that covered the earth and the thick clouds that sailed over peoples have been dispelled. Through the waters of baptism you have made us children of light. Guide us with your grace that we might do good deeds and proclaim your name with joy. We trust that one day you will raise us up in splendor, like Mary, to share the light of the kingdom, where you live and reign with Jesus and the Holy Spirit, one God, for ever and ever. Amen.

7. The Blessed Virgin Mary and the Presentation of the Lord
New Covenant

Scripture: Lo, I am sending my messenger
to prepare the way before me;
And suddenly there will come to the temple
the LORD whom you seek,
And the messenger of the covenant whom you desire.
Yes, he is coming, says the LORD of hosts.

(Mal 3:1)

Mass: Mal 3:1-4; Luke 2:27-35

Reflection: Even though the words of the prophet Malachi about sending a messenger to prepare the way are often predicated of John the Baptist, they can be aptly applied to Mary, the mother of Jesus. Indeed, if anyone prepared the way for the coming of the Lord, it was she.

Mary conceived the Word of God in her womb. For months she carried the Son, who would announce God's new covenant in his own blood. She gave the Word flesh; she was the chosen instrument for the incarnation. In this way, she prepared the way for the coming of the God-made-man into the world.

Through his suffering, death, and resurrection, Jesus established the new covenant in his own blood. Through their weekly celebration of Eucharist, Christians remember this new covenant and their participation in it through their own immersion in the waters of baptism, in which they died to an old way of life and were raised to the new way established by Jesus.

Like Mary, all Christians are now messengers of the covenant. They are messengers not necessarily by the words they speak or preach, but by the lives they lead. A Christian's lifestyle speaks more eloquently than the words which come forth from his or her mouth.

For example, when it is more convenient to tell a little white lie in order to protect one's reputation, the Christian who tells the whole truth witnesses to the new covenant of Jesus. There may be some suffering involved with the truth, but it is embraced because this person prefers to be a messenger of the truth rather than a messenger of deceit.

When a parent teaches a child to face up to the consequences of his or her actions, even if it entails some amount of punishment, that parent is teaching his or her child the way of the new covenant of Jesus. It might involve being cut from the team because of poor grades or because of poor study habits, but the lesson learned will never be forgotten, and it will shape a child for a lifetime.

Even the professional messengers of the covenant—priests, preachers, teachers—must be willing to make people uncomfortable at times and risk alienation in order to be faithful to the new covenant. It is difficult to remind people of their obligations week after week, but this is the task that the new covenant sets before them.

Every day God sends messengers to prepare the way for his coming into people's lives. Suddenly, without warning, one appears and announces the new covenant, the new way, of Jesus, who is always coming into the lives of people.

Meditation: Who has been a messenger of the covenant for you most recently? To whom have you been a messenger of the covenant most recently?

Prayer: God of the covenant, once you made an agreement with Abraham and Sarah; you promised them a new land, flowing with milk and honey. You kept your promise and made their descendants as numerous as the stars in the sky and the sand on the seashore. Through the blood of Jesus, your only-begotten Son, born

of Mary, you established a new covenant with all people. Continue
to send your messengers of this covenant that we might know what
you desire of us and put your will into action in our lives. We ask
this through our Lord Jesus Christ, who lives and reigns with you
and the Holy Spirit, one God, for ever and ever. Amen.

8. Our Lady of Nazareth
Option A: Home

Scripture: When they [Mary and Joseph] had fulfilled all the
prescriptions of the law of the Lord, they returned to Galilee, to
their own town of Nazareth (Luke 2:39).

Mass: Gal 4:4-7; Luke 2:22, 39-40 or Luke 2:41-52

Reflection: The word "home" is used in a variety of ways. In the
morning, a man leaves "home" to go to work. A woman may clean
her "home" during the day. Children return "home" after school
in the afternoon. Using the word "home" is these ways indicates
that a "home" is a place.

But "home," while referring to a definite place, also carries a
whole set of connotations. "Home" is security. When a child falls
down and skins his or her knee, that child runs for "home." The
security of a comforting parent or guardian is found in the "home."

For the parents who work all day, "home" means rest. In a
favorite easy chair or stretched out on the sofa, a parent rests after
a hard day's work. Coming "home" implies returning to an at-
mosphere of rest.

Sometimes, "home" can be understood as punishment. A teen-
age son or daughter is often grounded. This means that he or she
is confined to "home." Not being able to leave "home" makes
"home" like a jail.

Mary, the mother of Jesus, had a "home" in Nazareth. And
like all other people, the word carried definite connotations for her.
In her "home" she received the message of Gabriel and agreed to
become the mother of the Savior. In her "home" she raised Jesus
and nurtured him with the word of God, as it had been recorded

by Moses and the prophets. Mary's "home" was the place where the God of Israel chose to live in his incarnate form.

Everyone has a place named "home." Many memories are kept there. Much is associated with one's "home."

Meditation: Make a list of all of the connotations that the word "home" has for you.

Prayer: God of the home, you willed that the message of the birth of your Son should be delivered to Mary's home in Nazareth. In her home, the Virgin nourished her only child on your word. She taught him the hope of the prophets. Make our homes places where we can receive your word in faith. Give us security in the places where we live. Bring us one day to the eternal home where you live with our Lord Jesus Christ, your Son, and the Holy Spirit, one God, for ever and ever. Amen.

8. Our Lady of Nazareth
Option B: Clothes

Scripture: Put on then, as God's chosen ones, holy and beloved, heartfelt compassion, kindness, humility, gentleness, and patience, bearing with one another and forgiving one another, if one has a grievance against another; as the Lord has forgiven you, so must you also do. And over all these put on love, that is, the bond of perfection (Col 3:12-14).

Mass: Col 3:12-17; Matt 2:13-15, 19-23

Reflection: Every morning after waking up and getting out of bed most people shower and dress for the day ahead. Some thought might be given to what clothes one will wear for the day; it all depends on where one is going and what appointments one may have. However, little thought is given to putting on the clothes, as everyone knows how to dress.

There are other types of clothes beside those which protect and cover the body. These clothes are often referred to as virtues, but they are worn just as dresses and pants and shirts are. They are invisible most of the time, but they are manifest in how one person deals with another.

Heartfelt compassion is one type of these special clothes. A person who puts on heartfelt compassion is one who feels the pain of another with his or her heart. Sympathy springs from the depths of one's being and one understands another's suffering with one's heart.

Kindness is another type of clothes that some people wear. Kindness is demonstrated with an unrequested and unsolicited deed. A person is moved to assist another. At other times, kindness may be displayed with a few words that convey support.

Some people put on humility. This does not mean that they go around degrading themselves. It does mean that they have a healthy self-understanding. Humility reminds others that they are only passing through this world; they are not here to stay for ever. Humility reminds others that they are of the earth, and that some day they will return to the earth.

Other clothes such as gentleness, patience, and forgiveness can be worn. Likewise, the best clothing to put on is love. Love motivates people to be all that God has called them to be.

Mary wore clothes such as these. She put on heartfelt compassion, kindness, humility, gentleness, patience, forgiveness, and love. In Nazareth, she wore these clothes and wove them into the life of her Son, Jesus. Through the nurturing she gave to Jesus, she participated in God's work and love for the world.

Meditation: Besides the physical clothes that you put on every day, make a list of the other types of clothes that you wear.

Prayer: Lord God, you have made us your chosen ones, holy and beloved. Through the ministry of Jesus, your Son, born of Mary of Nazareth, you have clothed all humanity with your grace. Through the working of your Holy Spirit, clothe us with heartfelt compassion, kindness, humility, gentleness, patience, forgiveness, and love. Help us to follow Jesus to the perfection of the kingdom, where you live and reign with him and the Holy Spirit, one God, for ever and ever. Amen.

9. Our Lady of Cana
On Eagle Wings

Scripture: Moses went up the mountain to God. Then the LORD called to him and said, " . . . Tell the Israelites: You have seen for yourselves how I treated the Egyptians and how I bore you up on eagle wings and brought you here to myself. Therefore, if you hearken to my voice and keep my covenant, you shall be my special possession, dearer to me than all other people, though all the earth is mine" (Exod 19:3-5).

Mass: Exod 19:3-8; John 2:1-11

Reflection: When playing team sports as children, most people can remember an occasion of being chosen, picked to be a member of a team. Two captains were named, and they proceeded to call the names of the kids they wanted on their teams. Gradually the line of those who wanted to play dwindled. Whoever was last was always embarrassed, because this meant that he or she was not the best player.

When God chose Israel as his special possession, no one was last. Indeed, every person was chosen first. God engineered the great escape (exodus) of his people out of Egyptian slavery through the leadership of Moses. Like an eagle that soars on the air currents, God brought his people to Mount Sinai, where he could enter into a solemn covenant with them.

Israel accepted God's offer and became a chosen people. Israel entered into a solemn agreement with God and became a nation dearer to God than all the other people on the earth.

If this were not enough to convince people of their special status, God chose them again in the new covenant of the blood of his Son, Jesus. The first of Jesus' signs, according to the Gospel of John, took place during a wedding at Cana, where water was turned into wine. The mother of Jesus was in attendance.

Throughout John's Gospel the only other appearance of the mother of Jesus is at the cross, where water and blood flow from the side of Jesus after his death. The Church, the mother of all people, is born from the side of Christ. Mary, who represents the Church, is there. Through this death-birth, God once again chooses all people.

The water from the side of Christ continues to flow in the sacrament of baptism. One is plunged into the death-dealing waters and rises to share in the Body and Blood of Christ at the altar. The Church, a mother, both gives birth to her children and nourishes them with the word of God, the bread of life, and the cup of eternal salvation.

Meditation: In what ways has God brought you closer to himself? How did these experiences reveal the maternal dimension of God?

Prayer: God of the Exodus, on eagle wings you bore your people as you led them from Egyptian slavery to freedom. At Mount Sinai you entered into a covenant with Israel and promised her that she would be your special possession. In Jesus of Nazareth you entered into a new covenant with your people. Through the water and blood from his side you gave birth to your Church. Give us the grace to keep your covenant that we might join the mother of Jesus and all your saints in the kingdom where you live and reign with your Christ and the Holy Spirit, one God, for ever and ever. Amen.

Lenten Season

10. Holy Mary, Disciple of the Lord
Discipleship

Scripture: "Who is my mother? Who are my brothers?" And stretching out his hand toward his disciples, [Jesus] said, "Here are my mother and my brothers. For whoever does the will of my heavenly Father is my brother, and sister, and mother" (Matt 12:48-50).

Mass: Sir 51:13-18, 20-22; Luke 2:41-52 or Matt 12:46-50

Reflection: The author of each Gospel has his own perspective or understanding of the meaning of discipleship. Mark, for instance, thinks that discipleship is suffering abandonment. This is demonstrated by portraying all of Jesus' disciples as abandoning him before his death. Jesus is left to die alone, abandoned by all. Even the Markan Jesus thinks that God has abandoned him as he cries out, "My God, my God, why have you abandoned me?"

Luke has a different view of discipleship. For him, a disciple is one who hears the word of God and acts on it. Through his Gospel, Luke portrays the disciples of Jesus as those who listen to his teaching and then practice and preach what they hear. In this Gospel, Mary is portrayed as the most faithful disciple who hears God's word and then acts on it.

Matthew is interested in disciples who are willing to do the will of the heavenly Father. For Matthew those who are willing to be followers of Jesus' righteous path, even when this may mean the breaking of the Law, are in effect doing the will of God. These form the true family of Jesus.

While Mary is understood to be the physical mother of Jesus, anyone who does God's will can be understood as an extended mother of Jesus. By doing God's will, Mary is portrayed as a disciple. The follower of Jesus who does God's will is also a disciple.

Such discipleship often involves suffering and death. A follower of Jesus is not rescued from suffering and death, since these events are part of the definition of being human. However, what God does promise is that he will raise up those who do his will, because they are his faithful disciples. His promise is verified in Jesus, whom God raised from the dead.

Meditation: In what ways do you characterize yourself as a disciple of Jesus?

Prayer: Heavenly Father, you never cease to call men and women to be followers of your Son. Through him you have taught us to do your will. When we hear your word and put it into practice, we find that we are members of the true family of Jesus. Give us

the willingness of Mary to listen and to act. Give us the grace of
your Holy Spirit to help us to face the suffering and death that
discipleship involves. May we always trust in your promise of eternal life, which you share with Jesus and the Holy Spirit, one God,
for ever and ever. Amen.

11. The Blessed Virgin Mary at the Foot of the Cross I
Suffering

Scripture: If God is for us, who can be against us? He who did
not spare his own Son but handed him over for us all, how will
he not also give us everything else along with him (Rom 8:31-32)?

Mass: Rom 8:31-39; John 19:25-27

Reflection: Suffering is not an experience that is welcomed with
open arms by most people. Suffering, rather, is an experience which
is labeled as negative and to be avoided. Modern medicine produces
new drugs every day to alleviate suffering. Television commercials
provide information about diet programs which enable people to
lose weight without suffering from hunger. New homes, new cars,
new beds, etc., are all aimed at removing some type of human
suffering and replacing it with comfort.

The God of Christians, however, is a God of suffering. Rather
than being removed from human suffering, God demonstrated in
the birth of Jesus, born of the Virgin Mary, that he was interested
in experiencing suffering. God got into the flesh and blood of people
in order to understand their suffering. God became human in the
incarnation of Jesus in order to know the meaning of suffering.

Jesus, God's only-begotten Son, found suffering to be holy. Being human, Jesus did not go and actively seek out suffering, but
that which did confront him was embraced as holy. Jesus met suffering with love and wrapped his arms around it, kissed it, and made
it salvific. Through love, suffering was made redemptive.

By not sparing his own Son from everything that defines the
"human condition" except sin, God has made it possible for every

person to share in God's life for ever. Whatever suffering that may confront a person—cancer, AIDS, psychological stress, death—is holy. Through his or her suffering, an individual is wrapped in God's love. If the suffering of Jesus on the cross brought him closer to his Father, then the suffering of any follower of Christ can serve to do no more than bring him or her closer to God. Nothing can separate one from God.

Meditation: What kind of suffering have you recently experienced? How has it brought you closer to God?

Prayer: God of suffering, through the suffering, death, and resurrection of your Son we have come to understand the great love that you have for all people. Born of the Virgin Mary, he fully experienced the human condition. He taught us to embrace our suffering and to carry it to the cross. Because you did not spare him but handed him over for us, we trust that your love for us will sustain us through our daily trials. Give us the strength of Mary, who suffered at the foot of the cross of Jesus who lives and reigns with you and the Holy Spirit, one God, for ever and ever. Amen.

12. The Blessed Virgin Mary at the Foot of the Cross II
Hope

Scripture: [King] Uzziah said to [Judith]: "Blessed are you, daughter, by the Most High God, above all the women on earth; and blessed be the LORD God, the creator of heaven and earth, who guided your blow at the head of the chief of our enemies. Your deed of hope will never be forgotten by those who tell of the might of God" (Jdt 13:18-19).

Mass: Jdt 13:17-20; John 19:25-27

Reflection: The complete tale of the exploits of Judith can be found in the Hebrew Bible (Old Testament) Book of Judith. She is remembered for having tricked Holofernes, the general in charge of the Assyrian army, and for cutting off his head. Thus, a woman came to the rescue of Israel and defeated her enemies. A woman did what King Uzziah was unable to do!

The blessing which Uzziah uttered on Judith's behalf was applied to Mary, the mother of Jesus, by the author of Luke's Gospel. After Mary arrives at the home of Zechariah and Elizabeth, Elizabeth declares her to be blessed above all women.

Like Judith, Mary was guided by God. God led Judith in the plan to defeat her enemies and to cut off Holofernes' head. Judith was obedient to God and was the instrument which he used to save his people from the Assyrians.

Mary was led by God to accept a pregnancy without having known a man. She risked ostracization and death, but, nevertheless, she did the will of God. The mother of Jesus was the instrument which God used to save his people from their sins.

Judith's deed of hope is recorded in the book named after her. Her name and her honor live on. However, her name and her honor give praise and glory to God, the creator of heaven and earth, her guide.

Likewise, Mary's deed of hope lives on. Her Son, Jesus, is the subject of the entire New Testament. He suffered and died, but God raised him from the dead. Those who believe in him continue to await his return in glory and their own day of resurrection. Mary points toward the Christ, who gives his Father praise and glory by doing God's will.

Every Christian is called by God to do deeds of hope. Every person is responsible for rescuing those in the grips of poverty, freeing those held hostage by egoism, and helping those who are suffering through their final hours. By Judith's willingness to be led by God, she became a sign of hope. By Mary's willingness to be led by God, she gave birth to hope. By the Christian's willingness to follow Jesus and minister to those in need, he or she becomes a sign of hope in the midst of a world that is often hopeless.

Meditation: Identify one way that you have been a sign of hope for someone in the past. How can you be a sign of hope for someone today?

Prayer: Creator of heaven and earth, you led your chosen daughter, Judith, to victory over her enemies. You called your Virgin daughter, Mary, to give birth to the One who would defeat the enemy of sin. In Jesus, your Son, you gave incarnate hope to the world. Make of us signs of hope to those trapped in poverty, to those held prisoner to selfishness, and to those facing their imminent death. Guide our deeds that they might give praise to you, Father, Son, and Holy Spirit, one God, who lives and reigns for ever and ever. Amen.

13. The Commending of the Blessed Virgin Mary
Commendation

Scripture: It . . . happened that seven brothers with their mother were arrested and tortured with whips and scourges by the king, to force them to eat pork in violation of God's law. Most admirable and worthy of everlasting remembrance was the mother, who saw her seven sons perish in a single day, yet bore it courageously because of her hope in the LORD (2 Macc 7:1, 20).

Mass: 2 Macc 7:1, 20-29; John 19:25-27

Reflection: A person who is commended is entrusted with care of another. Parents commend their children to day care or to a baby sitter. Students are commended to their teachers. Often times older adults are commended to a nursing home.

At a time of persecution, the mother of seven sons commended her children to the care of God. This brave woman, rather than counsel her sons to save their lives and to renege on their faith, watched as each of them was put to death. She remained steadfast in hope in God.

Jesus, the son of Mary, was commended to his mother by God, his Father. The Virgin accepted the Word of God, carried him for months in her womb, and gave birth to him in the wonder of the incarnation. Jesus was entrusted to Mary's care until the day he began his mission of teaching and preaching about the kingdom of God.

According to the author of John's Gospel, Jesus commended his mother to the disciple whom he loved. While dying on the cross, Jesus entrusted the care of his mother, who appears only one other time in John's Gospel (at the wedding feast at Cana), to the Church, which was about to be born from water and blood pouring out of his pierced side.

Today, all people are commended to the Church, who is both the bride of Christ and mother of the faithful. Through the public proclamation of the word of God, people are nourished. Through the sacraments, people are fed. As a mother, the Church brings her children to birth through the Spirit-filled water. As a bride, she draws them into the intimate love of God in Christ Jesus.

Because the Church is the body of Christ, every member is responsible for commending every other member to God in prayer, through acts of charity, and by courageous witness of faith. Thus, like the mother of seven sons, people commend each other to God, as they wait in joyful hope for the return of Jesus.

Meditation: To whom have you recently been commended? Recently, who has been commended to you?

Prayer: God of hope, when your people suffered persecution and death, you taught them to place their hope for new life in you. You revealed the fullness of this life in Jesus, born of Mary of Nazareth. Make us witnesses of his resurrection. Enable us to commend each other to your constant care. Give us the hope that one day we may share in the kingdom, where you live and reign with him and the Holy Spirit, one God, for ever and ever. Amen.

14. The Blessed Virgin Mary, Mother of Reconciliation

Ambassadors

Scripture: All this is from God, who has reconciled us to himself through Christ and given us the ministry of reconciliation, namely, God was reconciling the world to himself in Christ, not counting their trespasses against them and entrusting to us the message of reconciliation. So we are ambassadors for Christ, as if God were appealing through us (2 Cor 5:18-20).

Mass: 2 Cor 5:17-21; John 19:25-27

Reflection: An ambassador is an official envoy or representative of another. Many countries have ambassadors in other countries. These men and women are the resident representatives of their own governments; they are appointed to share the concerns of their home countries with those in which they reside.

Paul understood himself as an ambassador, or a minister, of reconciliation. Paul was God's official representative to the Gentiles. He was called to be an apostle to share the good news about the righteousness that God had accomplished for people in Jesus. Through Paul, God was calling all people to accept his gift of reconciliation.

According to Paul, God's free gift to all people was unification. This oneness was brought about through the suffering, death, and resurrection of Jesus. God reconciled all people to himself through his own Son, Jesus, who was born of the Virgin Mary. Therefore, as the mother of Jesus, Mary is rightly referred to as the mother of reconciliation.

Today, every person is commissioned to continue to spread this good news. In other words, every human being is an ambassador of reconciliation. The message that God has canceled all transgressions is to be shared with the whole world.

It can begin at home with a kind word instead of an angry statement. It can spread to the work place with a listening ear of concern rather than with loose lips ready to spread every bit of gossip. Reconciliation can take place when people agree to disagree. In these and in many other ways, every person can demonstrate that he or she is an ambassador of God's reconciliation, which began in Christ and continues today.

Meditation: Identify one way that you have been an ambassador of reconciliation in the past week. Today, how can you be an ambassador of reconciliation?

Prayer: God of reconciliation, in Christ, your Son, you have made all things new. The old creation has passed away; now, we have been reborn through water and the Spirit. Your gift of the Reconciler, born of Mary, has brought us into the inner circle of your love. Make of us worthy messengers of your good news. Fill us with your grace that we might be true ambassadors of the reconciling love that you have lavished upon us. We ask this through our Lord Jesus Christ, your Son, who lives and reigns with you and the Holy Spirit, one God, for ever and ever. Amen.

Easter Season

15. The Blessed Virgin Mary and the Resurrection of the Lord

Earthquake

Scripture: After the sabbath, as the first day of the week was dawning, Mary Magdalene and the other Mary came to see the tomb. And behold, there was a great earthquake; for an angel of the Lord descended from heaven, approached, rolled back the stone, and sat upon it. His appearance was like lightning and his clothing was white as snow (Matt 28:1-3).

Mass: Rev 21:1-5; Matt 28:1-10

Reflection: An earthquake takes place when a trembling is caused by some volcanic or tectonic activity. Molten lava is coughed up from deep inside the stomach of the earth, and this retching causes the earth to quake. The great plates of the crust of the earth begin to shift and to slide one against another, and this rubbing makes the earth quake. Along fault lines (such as the San Andreas or New Madrid) earthquakes are common.

The report of the earthquake heralding the resurrection of Jesus is unique to Matthew's Gospel. It heralds the final age, God's definitive breakthrough and revelation in history. The earthquake represents the beginning of the end, something new.

Indeed, the resurrection of Jesus from the dead was something new. Jesus, the Son of God born of the Virgin Mary, died a criminal's death. He suffered capital punishment. But God raised Jesus from the dead and bestowed upon him new and eternal life. The new age of God's intervention in history began with this great and cosmic event.

Mary shared in her Son's resurrection from the dead. She, who had been chosen to be the mother of God, had already experienced an earthquake, so to speak, at his conception. God broke into her life with his light and wrapped her in the clothing of his grace, which was as white as snow. Because of her privileged place, she was deemed acceptable to share in God's new life brought about through the resurrection of Jesus even before God's final earth-shattering act. The angel of the Lord had already descended from heaven and rolled back the stone of sin before she was born. Furthermore, in the incarnation Mary's womb became the tomb of new life.

Today, earthquakes continue. These are not just of the physical types that shake up people and houses and spew molten rock into the heavens. God continues to break into people's lives with the power of an earthquake. When a long-awaited idea finally comes to birth, an earthquake takes place. When a marital problem is solved, the earth shakes. When the calm of trust descends upon a crisis situation, God has flooded people with his grace and a minor earthquake has occurred.

Meditation: When did you most recently experience an earthquake? Explain.

Prayer: God of earthquakes, you announced the coming of the new age with the resurrection of Jesus from the dead. Through the womb of the Virgin Mary, you brought forth the enfleshment of your grace, and, through the tomb, you established your enduring presence and new life with your people. Roll back the stone of unfaithfulness from our lives. Flash forth your lightning of faith. Clothe us in the whiteness of new life. On the last day grant that we might share in the kingdom, where you live and reign with Jesus and the Holy Spirit, one God, for ever and ever. Amen.

16. Holy Mary, Fountain of Light and Life
Fountain

Scripture: Jesus cried out and said, "Whoever believes in me believes not only in me but also in the one who sent me, and whoever sees me sees the one who sent me. I came into the world as light, so that everyone who believes in me might not remain in darkness" (John 12:44-46).

Mass: Acts 2:14, 36-40, 41-42; John 12:44-50 or John 3:1-6

Reflection: Fountains with flowing water can be found in gardens, surrounded by multiple-blossomed and various-colored plants. In hospital foyers, in mall center courts, and in church baptisteries fountains are frequently located. The flow of water is soothing and restful.

Mary, the mother of Jesus, can be referred to as a fountain. First, she is a fountain of light. In giving birth to her only Son, Jesus, she brought forth into the world the true light. She had already overflowed with God's light since she had been wrapped in grace from the moment of her conception. Like a fountain with leaping waters, she became the fountain of the Light, Jesus, for the world.

Second, Mary can be called the fountain of life. This can be understood in a physical sense, insofar as she carried her Son in her womb for months and then, like an overflowing fountain, gave birth to him. In a spiritual sense, Mary is the fountain of eternal life. Anyone who believes in Jesus and the Father who sent him will share in everlasting life.

For various reasons, many people prefer darkness and death to life. Human weakness leads people to sin. Alone, people are not capable of walking into light and life. So, God sent Jesus, who taught God's word. Jesus did not condemn the world, but offered everyone who believes the possibility of light and life.

Today, every Christian is commissioned to be another Mary, a fountain of light and life. By example, every individual emanates light or darkness. Through his or her mission, every person preaches Jesus' way. By participating actively in his or her ecclesial community, a person joins with others who overflow with the light and life of Christ.

Meditation: Most recently, how have you been a fountain of light and life? Explain.

Prayer: God of light and life, you sent your only-begotten Son, Jesus, into the world to preach your word. True man and true God, he was born of the Virgin Mary, whom you had prepared to be the mother and fountain of light and life. Open our ears to hear your word. Through your Holy Spirit give us understanding. Enable us to believe in Jesus, so that we might not remain in darkness but come to share in the fountain of eternal life. We ask this through our Lord Jesus Christ, who lives and reigns with you and the Holy Spirit, one God, for ever and ever. Amen.

17. Our Lady of the Cenacle
Witness

Scripture: [Jesus said to his apostles:] "You will receive power when the holy Spirit comes upon you, and you will be my witnesses in Jerusalem, throughout Judea and Samaria, and to the ends of the earth." When he had said this, as they were looking on, he was lifted up, and a cloud took him from their sight (Acts 1:8-9).

Mass: Acts 1:6-14; Luke 8:19-21

Reflection: The word "witness" comes from the Greek word for "martyr." A "martyr" was a person who "witnessed" to his or her faith to the point of being willing to die for what he or she believed. In other words, a "witness" is one who attests to the truth; he or she gives testimony that faith is more important than life itself.

The strength to "witness" to one's faith comes from the Holy Spirit, God's gift to the Church. When a person tells the truth instead of spreading gossip about another, he or she functions as a "witness." Such a deed may cost a reputation, but this type of "martyrdom" is more important than denying the good reputation of another human being.

When young people are able to "just say no" to drugs, alcohol, tobacco, or sex, they "witness" to the importance of health. There is a lot of peer pressure to join the group and to do what every one else is doing. Such "witnessing" may result in the "martyrdom" of ostracization, but isn't a long and healthy life worth more than a few moments of pleasure?

In many countries today people bear "witness" to their faith with their lives. In an attempt to help the poor, the alienated, the oppressed, and the downtrodden, some missionaries have been raped, killed, and thrown out of the host country. Such "witnessing" has resulted in "martyrdom," the literal shedding of blood for faith.

In a certain sense, Mary, the mother of Jesus, was a "witness." In giving birth to her Son, she shed blood. While observing his crucifixion and death on the cross, she was "martyred." Her strength came from the Holy Spirit, who had overshadowed her from the moment of her own conception. She, along with her Son's followers, awaited the fullness of strength that the Spirit bestowed, so that "witnessing" might continue to the ends of the earth.

Meditation: When have you most recently been a "witness"? Was any type of "martyrdom" involved? Explain.

Prayer: Father, you did not permit your only-begotten Son to sleep in death, for you raised him to new life on the third day. You fulfilled his promise and sent the Holy Spirit to strengthen all who believe in him, that they might be effective witnesses throughout the whole world. Pour out on us this special gift. Seal us with the courage we need to be your martyrs today. Overshadow us, as you did Mary, the mother of Jesus, who lives and reigns with you and the Holy Spirit, one God, for ever and ever. Amen.

18. The Blessed Virgin Mary, Queen of Apostles
Church

Scripture: When Jesus saw his mother and the disciple . . . whom he loved, he said to his mother, "Woman, behold, your son." Then he said to the disciple, "Behold, your mother" (John 19:26-27).

Mass: Acts 1:12-14, 2:1-4; John 19:25-27

Reflection: In John's Gospel, the Virgin Mary is never referred to by name; she is always called the mother of Jesus. Furthermore, she makes only two appearances in the whole Gospel: at the wedding at Cana and at the foot of the cross. By portraying her in these two scenes, the author has established her as an image of the Church.

As at Cana, Jesus addresses his mother as "woman" when he is crucified. She represents the Church, given to the followers of Jesus (represented by the beloved disciple), who in turn are entrusted to her care.

At Cana, the water in six stone jars became wine. The jars were numbered as six because all was still incomplete. Now, from the cross the pierced side of Jesus pours forth blood and water. The sign of blood is a reminder both of the wine at Cana and the blood of the covenant, which was sealed between Moses and God. Jesus gives his own blood in the Eucharist under the sign of wine as nourishment for the Church, his mother.

The sign of water is a reminder of the necessity to be born again of water and Spirit, as Jesus told Nicodemus. It is the water that quenched the thirst of the Samaritan woman. It is the fountain that leaps up to provide eternal life. It is the seventh, complete, jar from Cana.

At Cana, Jesus declares to his mother that his hour has not yet come. His hour came when he was raised up in glory on the cross. As he reigns from such an unusual throne, he makes his mother a sign of the Church to which he gives birth from his own side. She who had given him life is now entrusted with the life of all. The mother of Jesus, the Church, becomes the mother of all of those who are baptized into eternal life and have their thirst satisfied with the best wine.

Meditation: Name three ways in which the Church has functioned as a mother for you.

Prayer: God of Jesus, you willed that your only-begotten Son be born of a woman. From the moment of her conception, you preserved Mary from any stain of sin. At the cross, Jesus made her the sign of the Church, the mother of all the people to whom he had given birth from his pierced side. Through the waters of baptism, you have made us members of your family. With the best of wine you satisfy our thirst. Keep us faithful to our baptismal promises, and give us a share in the eternal wedding feast with Jesus, who lives and reigns with you and the Holy Spirit, one God, for ever and ever. Amen.

Ordinary Time: Section 1
19. Holy Mary, Mother of the Lord
Ark

Scripture: David assembled all Israel in Jerusalem to bring the ark of the LORD to the place which he had prepared for it. . . . The Levites bore the ark of God on their shoulders with poles, as Moses had ordained according to the word of the LORD (1 Chr 15:3, 15).

Mass: 1 Chr 15:3-4, 15-16; 16:1-2; Luke 1:39-47

Reflection: The ark was a special box, which contained the tablets of the Law, Moses' staff, and a jar of manna. For the Israelites, this special box was a sign of God's presence with his people. David brought the ark to Jerusalem, once he had captured the city and made it his capital. There, the ark was placed in a special tent. Later, Solomon, David's son, built the Temple in which the ark was placed in the innermost shrine, the Holy of Holies. Thus, God lived with his people.

Mary, the mother of Jesus, is an ark. Because she consented to conceive the Son of God in her womb and give him flesh and life, she became the ark of God's presence. Like the box of old, which, in a sense, contained God, Mary carried the Son of God in her womb. She gave birth to him who is the human image of God. When the historical Temple was destroyed, the ark was lost. However, when the body of Jesus was destroyed on the cross, God raised him to new life. Now, the Church, the new body of Christ, is the ark of God's presence. Every person who is born again of water and Spirit is a member of the ark of the Church.

Just as Mary gave birth to Jesus for the salvation of the world, so every Christian is entrusted with the task of spreading the good news that he taught. Through their preaching, Christians speak of the great things that God has done and continues to do. Through their teaching, Christians instruct others in the ways of God. Through their lifestyle, Christians bear witness to the great truths of their faith.

At one time, God took up residence in the ark. Then, God came to live in the flesh and blood of Jesus, his only-begotten Son. Now, God lives in the Church, the body of Christ, the ark of God's presence.

Meditation: In what ways are you like an ark, bearing the presence of God to others?

Prayer: God of David, you chose the ark as a sign of your presence with your people, Israel. In the fullness of time, you chose the body of Jesus, born of Mary, to be the sign of your love for your people. Now, you make your dwelling in the hearts of the members of the Church, the body of Christ. Make us aware of your constant love. Help us to live according to your ways. Enable us to be signs of your presence in our world. We ask this through our Lord Jesus Christ, your Son, who lives and reigns with you and the Holy Spirit, one God, for ever and ever. Amen.

20. Holy Mary, the New Eve
Marriage

Scripture: On the third day there was a wedding in Cana in Galilee, and the mother of Jesus was there. Jesus and his disciples were also invited to the wedding (John 2:1-2).

Mass: Rev 21:1-5; Luke 1:26-38 or John 2:1-11

Reflection: A wedding is an occasion for a celebration. Relatives and friends of the bride and the groom gather around the couple to witness to their making of vows and to support them in their new course for their lives. Some type of reception, in which the couple are honored, usually follows the marriage ceremony.

The people of Israel were considered to be God's bride. The covenant, which God entered into with his people, was the marriage vow—God would be their God and they would be his people. This unique union of God and people was remembered and celebrated every time a man and woman joined hands in marriage.

The first sign of Jesus, according to John's Gospel, takes place during a marriage celebration. The water is turned into wine to save the newly-married couple from embarrassment. But there is another marriage celebration that John portrays. This new union is between Jesus and the Church.

Jesus is the new Adam, who does his Father's will. Mary is the new Eve, who also does God's will. Instead of tempting Adam to eat of the tree of knowledge of good and evil, like the first Eve did, the new Eve simply informs Jesus that the old wine has been consumed. When his initial response is that the hour—the moment of glory—has not yet arrived, she merely instructs the servants to do whatever Jesus tells them.

Mary points toward her Son, the Christ. She indicates that the will of God is to be done. Through her obedience to God, she has already undone the disobedience of the first Eve. Through Jesus' obedience, he will undo the disobedience of the first Adam. Even before all this is accomplished, according to the Gospel of John's story line, the new marriage between God and people has taken place.

The fullness of the sign of water made wine will be revealed on the cross after Jesus has died. From his side will flow a stream of water and blood. He will give his life for his bride, the Church.

Meditation: Identify three ways that a married couple you know is a sign of the love that God has for all people.

Prayer: God of marriage, in your covenant with your people you bound yourself in love. Through Jesus, your Son, you renewed your marriage vows and sealed them with his blood. Keep us faithful to our promises. Enable us, like Mary, to point the way toward Jesus. May we one day share in the new wine and the wedding feast of the kingdom, where you live and reign with Jesus and the Holy Spirit, one God, for ever and ever. Amen.

21. The Holy Name of the Blessed Virgin Mary
Name

Scripture: The angel Gabriel was sent from God to a town of Galilee called Nazareth, to a virgin betrothed to a man named Joseph, of the house of David, and the virgin's name was Mary (Luke 1:26-27).

Mass: Sir 24:17-21; Luke 1:26-38

Reflection: The name of an object, a place, or a person identifies it. If a person in a kitchen asks for a plate, he or she will usually receive a flat dish. If one begins to talk about the Grand Canyon, everyone listening will mentally focus on the state of Arizona. Likewise, when someone shouts, "John!" a man bearing this name will stop and turn around to see who it is who called him.

Almost everything and everyone has a name. Sometimes this is for convenient reference; other times, knowing the name gives people a type of power over the object or the person. Whatever the reason, a name is important.

The mother of Jesus had a name—Mary. Hers was not a revolutionary name; indeed, it was a common name. Most likely, it came from her ancestor, Miriam, the sister of Moses and Aaron. The name Miriam means "beloved."

Indeed, Mary is a fitting name for the mother of Jesus. She was the "beloved" of God. God chose her to be the mother of his only-begotten Son. To her God entrusted the name of his Son—Jesus.

Therefore, it is fitting that Mary's name be honored. She, like her ancestor Miriam, made her name a holy name. God declared her "beloved," "favored," and "full of grace." She became the mother of the Son of the Most High.

Meditation: What is the meaning of your name? In what ways do you give honor to your name?

Prayer: God of Mary, once you refused to give your name to your servant, Moses. However, to the Virgin of Nazareth, you revealed the name of your Son. You wrapped her in your grace and prepared her to be a worthy mother. You made her your beloved. Pour out on us the grace of your·love. Enable us to know your will and to do it. May we always honor your name and make it known throughout the earth. We ask this through our Lord Jesus Christ, your Son, who lives and reigns with you and the Holy Spirit, one God, for ever and ever. Amen.

22. Holy Mary, Handmaid of the Lord
Handmaid

Scripture: Once [Samuel] was weaned, [Hannah] brought him up with her, along with a three-year-old bull, and ephah of flour, and a skin of wine, and presented him at the temple of the LORD in Shiloh. . . . Hannah . . . approached Eli and said: . . . "I prayed for this child, and the LORD granted my request. Now I, in turn, give him to the LORD; as long as he lives, he shall be dedicated to the LORD" (1 Sam 1:24-25, 27-28).

Mass: 1 Sam 1:24-28; 2:1-2, 4-8; Luke 1:26-38

Reflection: A handmaid is a personal maid or female servant. The function of a handmaid is to to serve her employer, to be at her employer's beck and call, and to be willing to do her employer's will.

One model handmaid is Hannah, wife of Elkanah and mother of Samuel. Like other Hebrew Bible (Old Testament) women, Hannah was sterile. However, as a servant of her God, she was willing to do whatever God asked of her. Her prayer was that she would conceive a son; her promise was that she would dedicate him to God. Even the name which she gave to her son—Samuel—indicated her willingness to serve God. Samuel means "name of God."

In the New Testament, Mary is the handmaid of God. According to Luke's Gospel, she twice declares her willingness to do God's will. First, after she receives the invitation to conceive the child, she says that she is God's servant. Second, after visiting Elizabeth, in a canticle she declares that God has looked upon her, his handmaid's, lowliness.

Like Hannah and Mary, every person is invited by God to be his handmaid. As demonstrated in Jesus, Son of Mary, every person is to be a servant of God. People are invited to do God's will.

Hannah did God's will by dedicating her son to God. God made Samuel a prophet to his people and a leader of Israel. It was Samuel who anointed Saul as the first king of the Israelites. It was Samuel who anointed David as Israel's second king.

Mary did God's will by conceiving and giving birth to the Son of God. He, in turn, preached and demonstrated that the greatest people are those who are willing to be servants, handmaids. His call was to everyone to follow in his footsteps.

Today, every time someone volunteers to work a few hours in the local soup kitchen, he or she is being a servant. When an individual reaches out with a visit to a nursing home, he or she is serving God in the person of another. Simply saying a prayer that one might know God's will and be able to do it is declaring that one is willing to be God's handmaid.

Meditation: In what ways have you functioned as God's handmaid during the past week?

Prayer: God of Hannah and Mary, you bestow the status of hand-maid upon those who are willing to serve you. In her old age you gave Hannah a child, the prophet Samuel, who anointed the kings of your people. In her youth you gave Mary your only-begotten Son, Jesus, who was the Anointed One, your servant. Give us your Spirit of discernment. Help us to know your will and to be eager in doing it. Mold us into faithful handmaids, that we might serve others as we wait for the coming in glory of Jesus, who lives and reigns with you and the Holy Spirit, one God, for ever and ever. Amen.

23. The Blessed Virgin Mary, Temple of the Lord
Temple Reverence

Scripture: The priests brought the ark of the covenant of the LORD to its place beneath the wings of the cherubim in the sanctuary, the holy of holies of the temple. . . . When the priests left the holy place, the cloud filled the temple of the LORD so that the priests could no longer minister because of the cloud, since the LORD's glory had filled the temple of the LORD (1 Kgs 8:6, 10-11).

Mass: 1 Kgs 8:1, 3-7, 9-11 or Rev 21:1-5; Luke 1:26-38

Reflection: The first Temple in Jerusalem was built by Solomon, King David's son and successor to the throne. Once the people of Israel ceased to be nomads living in tents and began to be a settled people living in houses, it was only logical that the tent of God's dwelling be turned into the house of God's dwelling. Thus, David prepared and hoped to build the Temple, but he was unable to get the project underway. Finally, Solomon built the Temple and brought the ark of the covenant into its innermost shrine.

The Temple was God's dwelling place with people; it was the house in which God lived. Therefore, it was a sacred place. The sign of God's taking up residence in the Temple was the cloud of incense, which filled the inner shrine where the ark was enthroned.

Mary, the mother of Jesus, is often called the temple of God because she became the dwelling place of God in human form. Just as Solomon prepared the Temple in every detail, so God prepared Mary to be the mother of Jesus. From the first moment of her conception she was preserved from any stain of sin and guided by the cloud of God's presence.

When she conceived Jesus in her own womb, she became a true temple, the dwelling place of God in the flesh. She carried this temple with her for months, until she gave birth to God-made-man.

Through the death and resurrection of Mary's Son, every person has been made a temple of God. In Baptism, the Spirit of God comes to live in everyone. In Confirmation, one is sealed again with this same Spirit. Every time the baptized gather for Eucharist, they pray that the Spirit will bind them together and make of them a living temple that praises God.

As a temple, a dwelling place for God, every person should reverence every other person. One temple should recognize the presence of the Lord in every other temple. By listening attentively, instead of thinking about what response one will make, a person can reverence God in another. By reaching out with an offer to lend a hand with a project, one person reverences God's presence in another. People can reverence God by recognizing the equal human dignity of every person on the earth no matter what the color of his or her skin.

Because people are made in the image and likeness of God, every person reveals a different dimension or aspect of God. To reverence the personhood of another is to worship God in the temple which that person is.

Meditation: In which human temples have you worshiped God during the past week?

Prayer: Lord God, once you chose to live in a tent with your people in the desert. After Solomon completed the building of the Temple in Jerusalem, you made that house your residence. In the fullness of time, you came to live among us in the person of Jesus, your Son, born of the Virgin Mary. Help us to recognize your presence in every person we meet. Give us a reverence for every life that you have created. Come and make your dwelling place in our hearts. We ask this through our Lord Jesus Christ, your Son, who

lives and reigns with you and the Holy Spirit, one God, for ever
and ever. Amen.

24. The Blessed Virgin Mary, Seat of Wisdom
Treasure

Scripture: Mary kept all these things, reflecting on them in her
heart (Luke 2:19).

Mass: Prov 8:22-31 or Sir 21:1-4, 8-12, 18-21; Matt 2:1-12 or
Luke 2:15-19 or Luke 10:38-42

Reflection: A hunt for a secret treasure never ceases to get people
enthusiastically involved. Treasure is the stuff of pirate movies. Finding treasure is the goal of deep sea divers, who look for ancient,
sunken ships. Being able to read the map with the X on it is supposed to lead a person to the treasure of a gold mine in the old
West. Even an Easter egg hunt is a treasure hunt.

Another type of treasure consists of memories. A man and
woman share their treasure as they remember their years of dating,
child-rearing, and job-hunting. Special birthdays, anniversaries, and
dinners are stored in the treasure box of one's memory. The days
of a fatal accident or the remembrance of the wrinkles of a favorite
grandparent are memory-treasures.

The ability to keep the memories of one's life as a treasure is
what makes a person wise. True wisdom means that one can call
forth from one's storehouse of memories the events of the past that
have shaped one and taught one the truth of living. Wisdom is
the product of years of remembering.

Mary, the mother of Jesus, kept the events of her Son as a treasure. She remembered the events of his conception and birth, as
only a mother could, and she pondered them, not always knowing their meaning. In her heart, she reflected on these events, and
this is what made her wise.

In the hectic world of today with all of its means of communi-
cation bombardment it is easy to forget and easier to not reflect
on the events of one's life. The failure to do so means that inevita-

bly one will repeat the mistakes of the past. The person who wants to be wise must take time each day to sit in silence, to open the treasure of memories, and to reflect on them in one's heart.

Meditation: What three memories in your treasure chest need to be reflected on today?

Prayer: God of memories, you never forget any of your people. When Israel was in slavery, you remembered her and led her to freedom. When your people sinned, you did not forget them, but called them home. Mary gave birth to your only Son, Jesus, who is the greatest sign of your love for the world and our greatest treasure. Teach us true wisdom as we remember him, what he taught, and how he died. Guide the reflection in our hearts with your Holy Spirit, who lives and reigns with you and our Lord Jesus Christ, one God, for ever and ever. Amen.

25. The Blessed Virgin Mary, Image and Mother of the Church I
Life-Giver

Scripture: The man called his wife Eve, because she became the mother of all the living (Gen 3:20).

Mass: Gen 3:9-15, 20; John 19:25-27

Reflection: The mythical account of the creation of the first man and woman says that the woman was named Eve, because she was to become the mother of any human being that ever came to life. In Hebrew, her name is derived from the word for life. Thus, her name describes her function as a giver of life.

While in the majority of cases in the animal world the female carries the animal until it is ready to be born or sits on the eggs waiting for them to hatch, the concept of life-giver can be expanded. Every person, no matter whether female or male, is responsible for giving life.

A person's life is shared in friendships. Going over the daily routine with a friend helps to soothe the struggle and to foster life. A picnic with people for whom one has a great concern is an opportunity for sharing life in a relaxed way. A dinner with soft background music and a good bottle of wine certainly supports life.

A husband and wife vow that they will share their lives with each other. In moments of silence, they support each other's life's work. In moments of intimacy, they give to each other all that they are. When bringing forth a child, they share life with each other and with the child who is conceived because of their life-giving marriage.

Priests share their lives with the people entrusted to their care. They preach the word of God. They celebrate the sacraments. Sometimes they spend hours just listening and comforting. All of these ministries amount to living-giving activities.

Mary, the mother of Jesus, is often referred to as the new Eve because she restored life to a fallen world. The first Eve gave life to the human race. The second Eve, Mary, gave birth to the giver of life, Jesus, the Son of God. He, in turn, shared the gift of eternal life with everyone who was willing to follow him.

The mystery which Jesus taught is that the more life is given and shared the more there is to give away and to share. By dying on the cross, Jesus gave all of his life. But the Father raised Jesus from the dead and enabled him to give an even better gift of eternal life.

Meditation: Identify three ways that you have given life to others today.

Prayer: God of life, from the rib of Adam's side you created Eve, the mother of all the living. From among all women, you chose Mary to give life to your only-begotten Son, Jesus, who bestowed upon the world the gift of eternal life. Give us a greater reverence for all life. Breathe into us the life-giving Spirit that we might be strengthened during our pilgrimage on earth. One day bring us to the joys of eternal life in the kingdom, where you live with our Lord Jesus Christ and the Holy Spirit, one God, for ever and ever. Amen.

26. The Blessed Virgin Mary, Image and Mother of the Church II

Prayer

Scripture: [The apostles] returned to Jerusalem . . . [and] went to the upper room where they were staying. . . . All these devoted themselves with one accord to prayer, together with some women, and Mary the mother of Jesus, and his brothers (Acts 1:12-14).

Mass: Acts 1:12-14; John 2:1-11

Reflection: Usually, when people hear the word "prayer," they think of saying prayers, such as the Hail Mary or the Our Father. Others may think about making the responses during the celebration of the Eucharist or singing hymns. Some people may even think of the prayers they read out of a book as part of their daily devotional lives.

Another way to understand the word "prayer" is to look at it from the perspective of what God does instead of what people do. The examples given above focus on something that people do. From God's perspective, insofar as we can imagine this, prayer is what God does in people.

Yes, God prays in human beings. God does not say words, make responses, or read out of a book. Rather, God speaks to a person from the depths of his or her heart, in the innermost secrets of his or her conscience. In this way, God urges the person toward the best type of life.

This is, obviously, the more difficult of the two types of prayer. It requires a quiet setting. It takes much time. A trained ear is absolutely necessary. Finally, courage to act on what one hears is demanded.

Community prayer can also provide the opportunity for God to speak. When groups of people gather to pray, they open up the possibility that God will speak to each of them through each other. The unity of those at prayer—saying prayers, singing hymns, or sitting quietly—imitates that of the apostles of Jesus and his mother after his ascension.

The apostles, Mary, and some other women gathered in prayer in the upper room. They were united in waiting for the gift of the Holy Spirit. They were there in obedience to Jesus' instruction and in the hope that they would receive renewed faith, courage, and direction for their lives. Their hopes were realized when the Spirit began to pray in them and send them on their mission to the ends of the earth.

Meditation: In the past week, in what ways have you prayed? In what ways has God prayed in you?

Prayer: Father of Jesus, you have taught your people to open their hearts to the fullness of the Holy Spirit, who will pray in them. Your gift to the world fills us with faith and courage and gives direction to our lives. Give us the quiet of the sunrise and the silence of the sunset that we might listen to your word. Gather us together into the community of believers of your Son, like the apostles and Mary, his mother, that we might learn from each other what you will for each of us. Make us the dwelling place of the Spirit, who lives and reigns with you and our Lord Jesus Christ, one God, for ever and ever. Amen.

27. The Blessed Virgin Mary, Image and Mother of the Church III
Bride

Scripture: I . . . saw the holy city, a new Jerusalem, coming down out of heaven from God, prepared as a bride adorned for her husband. I heard a loud voice from the throne saying, ''Behold, God's dwelling is with the human race'' (Rev 21:2-3).

Mass: Rev 21:1-5; Luke 1:26-38

Reflection: In an age where women demand that they receive the same rights and opportunities as men, it is strange that the focus of a wedding ceremony is still the bride. Traditions such as the groom not seeing the bride until the wedding on their marriage day, the giving-away of the bride by her father or another designated father figure, the veiling of the bride, her solemn march down the center aisle of the church, and the tossing of her bouquet and garter take a long time to change.

This image of the bride is used as a metaphor by the author of the Book of Revelation to describe the Church, the body of Christ, the people of God. The Church is God's bride. God has been joined in a covenant of love to his people through the birth, suffering, and death of his own Son, Jesus. Through the incarnation, God came to live with his bride. Through the suffering and death of Jesus, God renewed the marriage vows and sealed them in the new covenant of the body and blood of Christ.

Mary is a type of the Church, since God married her. From the first moment of her conception, God prepared Mary to be his bride. When she was about to be joined to Joseph, her betrothed, God stole her away from him, and, through the overshadowing of the Holy Spirit, placed the life of his only-begotten Son in her womb. Her willingness to do the will of God along with her faithfulness makes her a model of what the Church, the entire people of God, should strive to be.

Through baptism every person is immersed into the Church. Through the death-dealing waters every person dies to an old life and is raised up to a new life as a member of the body of Christ, God's bride. By imitating Mary's faithfulness, a person can continue to keep the marriage vows between God and his people.

Meditation: Make a list of the characteristics that you think should be found in every bride. How does each of these apply to the Church, God's bride?

Prayer: God of the new heaven and the new earth, once you made a covenant with your people in the desert and sealed it in blood. When your people wandered far away, you did not abandon them but renewed your promise in the blood of Jesus. You have made the Church, his body, your bride, and you have given us Mary as a model of what the Church is called to be. Make us obedient to your word. Keep us faithful to the covenant. Be with us always as we wait for the fullness of the kingdom, where you live and reign with our Lord Jesus Christ and the Holy Spirit, one God, for ever and ever. Amen.

28. The Immaculate Heart of the Blessed Virgin Mary
Kept in the Heart

Scripture: [Jesus said to his parents,] "Why were you looking for me? Did you not know that I must be in my Father's house?" But they did not understand what he said to them. He went down with them and came to Nazareth, and was obedient to them; and his mother kept all these things in her heart (Luke 2:49-51).

Mass: Jdt 13:17-20; 15:9; Luke 11:27-28 or Luke 2:46-51

Reflection: Even though from a biological point of view it is known that people use their brains to think, they locate their thoughts in their hearts. If a person is asked why he or she is sad, the reply may be, "I have a heavy heart." When a couple, who has been dating for a period of time, breaks up, either one or both of the parties might say, "I have a broken heart." After having reached a major decision after much thought, a person can be heard to say, "I feel this is right in my heart." The person who cannot sympathize with another is often told, "Get a heart."

Again, conscience, the ability to discern what is right and wrong behavior, occurs in the brain, but it is located in the heart. One's ability to be rational is a function of thinking, but most people speak of it as if the heart did it. "From the depths of my heart, I know this is the right thing to do," a person may say.

Mary, the mother of Jesus, was a woman who pondered the great things of God in her heart. With an immaculate heart, she conceived the Son of God; she was obedient to God's word. With a mother's love, she nourished his life with her own. With the wonder of a disciple, she listened to his words and observed his actions and stored all these things in her heart.

Those who follow Jesus have Mary as an example. When they fail to understand exactly what it is that God wants, they enter into the experience anyway, knowing that the fullness of the truth will be revealed later. When relationships seem to fall apart, they trust that the covenant of love with God remains firm. In the face of death, they stand firm with a hope in the resurrection.

The myriad events of life are kept in one's heart. These memories serve both as a teacher as life progresses and as a storehouse of remembrances of what God continues to do for those who are faithful.

Meditation: Bring forth three memories from your heart. What has each of these taught you? What do you remember that God did for you?

Prayer: Father of Jesus, you willed that your only-begotten Son be born of the Virgin Mary. You prepared her for this special privilege by wrapping her in your grace. She learned from the great events of the life of her Son and kept these things in her heart. Give us hearts like Mary's. Make us obedient to your word. Fill us with the Spirit of eagerness to do your will. We ask this through our Lord Jesus Christ, your Son, who lives and reigns with you and the Holy Spirit, one God, for ever and ever. Amen.

29. The Blessed Virgin Mary, Queen of All Creation

Royalty

Scripture: For a child is born to us, a son is given us;
　　　upon his shoulder dominion rests.
　　They name him Wonder-Counselor, God-Hero,
　　　Father-Forever, Prince of Peace.
　　His dominion is vast
　　　and forever peaceful.

(Isa 9:5-6)

Mass: Isa 9:1-3, 5-6; Luke 1:26-38

Reflection: A queen is a female monarch. In a true monarchy, if the queen has a husband, usually referred to as a king, then she is second in command. If she is the rightful heir to the throne, then she is the sole ruler of her country.

When the title of queen is given to Mary, the mother of Jesus, it refers to her reign in God's kingdom. Because she heard the word of God and did it, she shares in the eternal life of her Son. Because she said ''Yes'' to God's will, she has inherited a special place in his kingdom.

Jesus is given the title of king because he rules over the universe. God has given him a share of his own authority. With wisdom and prudence he rules over the Church, his body. Through his suffering and death on the cross, he displayed his love for his people and established a reign of peace. Because of his willingness to do his Father's will, he was crowned king of the universe. His mother became the queen.

However, Jesus' and Mary's royalty is meant to be shared with every member of the Church. What God did for Mary—raise her up to share in eternal life—is what God promises to do for everyone who remains in faithful service to his Son, Christ the King. Jesus was raised from the dead to share forever in new life. The royalty of the kingdom of God awaits every person who remains faithful to Jesus.

Mary stands as a model disciple. She gave birth to the hoped-for messianic king, who sits on David's throne and offers new life to those who live according to his way.

Meditation: In what ways do you already share in God's kingdom?

Prayer: Wonder-Counselor, God-Hero, Father-Forever, Prince of Peace, you have given us Jesus, born of Mary, to be our king and ruler. He has given us Mary to be our queen and example of faithfulness. Guide us with your Holy Spirit that we might be able to discern your will in our lives, willingly embrace it, and joyfully do it. Give us a share in the royalty of the kingdom, where you live and reign with our Lord Jesus Christ, your Son, and the Holy Spirit, one God, for ever and ever. Amen.

Ordinary Time: Section 2

30. The Blessed Virgin Mary, Mother and Mediatrix of Grace
Mediator

Scripture: The king stretched forth the golden scepter to Esther. So she rose and, standing in his presence, said: "If it pleases your majesty and seems proper to you, and if I have found favor with you and you love me, let a document be issued to revoke the letters which that schemer Haman . . . wrote for the destruction of the Jews in all the royal provinces" (Esth 8:4-5).

Mass: Esth 8:3-8, 16-17; John 2:1-11

Reflection: Christ is the sole mediator between God and people. Jesus brought about a renewed unity between God and people. His mediatorship is unique in the history of the world, since he is the Son of God.

However, God chooses to share in lesser degrees the role of mediator with other people. In this capacity Mary can rightly be called a mediatrix of grace. As a member of the body of Christ, she intercedes for people and prays for them to God. Like Queen Esther, she requests that God pour forth even more grace upon his people.

Mary is able to function as lesser mediator than Christ because she willingly conceived him in her womb, which God had prepared since her own conception. She was wrapped in God's grace and gave birth to God's only-begotten Son, the enfleshment of grace. She listened attentively to the word of God and put it into practice in her own flesh and blood.

Her mother's love is what motivates her to function as a mediator on behalf of her sisters and brothers in the Church. She, who cared for the Christ, continues to care for the members of his body; she teaches them forgiveness; she motivates reconciliation; she urges them to enter into prayer.

However, this unique mediatorship of Jesus and Mary's particular role as mediator do not exclude any follower of Jesus. Indeed, every Christian by the fact of his or her baptism and incorporation in the body of Christ is a mediator. Each person is obliged to offer forgiveness to the other members of the Church. Every Christian is a minister of reconciliation. Every member of the body of Christ prays for every other member. In these and in many other ways all people share in the role of mediator.

Meditation: During the past week, in what ways have you functioned as a mediator?

Prayer: God of Esther, when your servant implored King Ahasuerus, you moved him to grant her request. You have given us your only-begotten Son, Jesus, born of the Virgin Mary, to be our sole mediator with you, but you have also given all of us a share in this function. With a mother's love, Mary watches over us, her sisters and brothers in the Church. With this same type of love, you call us to forgiveness, reconciliation, and prayer. Guide us with the Holy Spirit and teach us never to allow ourselves to be separated from the grace given to us by our Lord Jesus Christ, who lives and reigns with you and the Holy Spirit, one God, for ever and ever. Amen.

31. The Blessed Virgin Mary, Fountain of Salvation
Option A: Water

Scripture: He brought me back to the entrance of the temple, and I saw water flowing out from beneath the threshold of the temple toward the east. . . . Along both banks of the river, fruit trees of every kind shall grow; their leaves shall not fade, nor their fruit fail. Every month they shall bear fresh fruit, for they shall be watered by the flow from the sanctuary (Ezek 47:1, 12).

Mass: Ezek 47:1-2, 8-9, 12; John 19:25-37

Reflection: Water sustains life. Without water people die. A group of people who had spent most of its existence in a desert would use water as a sign of abundance. Thus, Ezekiel's vision of water flowing from the Temple became a sign to the Israelites of paradise. It was a promise from God that one day God's people will be blessed as richly and abundantly as the first man and first woman in the paradisiacal garden.

So great will this blessing be that whatever fruit trees grow near the water will produce every month. In other words, the water will be effective; it will bring about the abundant blessings which are promised by God.

God kept his promise in Jesus, born of Mary of Nazareth. Jesus is the source of God's blessing. He is like a stream from God; whoever believes in him and follows him finds the way to eternal life. Those who live according to his ways discover that they produce the fruit of good works all the time.

Because Mary conceived God's only Son and gave him human life, she can be called a fountain of salvation. She gave the world the source of its new life. She had been prepared for this deed by God, who sent his stream of grace to her from the moment of her conception.

People come to share in this life-giving water in baptism. As they are immersed into the Spirit-filled water, they die to an old way of life and rise to a new life which overflows with the spring of God's grace. They drink from the stream which flows from the new temple of the body of Christ, the Church.

Every day the stream of God's grace continues to flow into a person's life. Out of every life God brings forth an abundance of good works and offers his gift that leads to eternal life.

Meditation: During the past week, what good works has God caused to flow in your life?

Prayer: God of the water, your stream of grace flows from your heavenly temple to every corner of the universe. Those who hear and follow your Son, born of the Virgin Mary, drink freely of your gift and produce abundantly. Through the work of the Holy Spirit in our lives, make us fruitful. Help us to spread the good news of Jesus, to remain his faithful followers, and to become fountains overflowing with the eternal life he shares with you and the Holy Spirit, one God, for ever and ever. Amen.

31. The Blessed Virgin Mary, Fountain of Salvation
Option B: Garden

Scripture: You are an enclosed garden, my sister, my bride,
an enclosed garden, a fountain sealed.
You are a park that puts forth pomegranates,
with choice fruits. . . .
You are a garden fountain, a well of water
flowing fresh from Lebanon.

(Song 4:12-13, 15)

Mass: Song 4:6-7, 9, 12-15; John 7:37-39

Reflection: Almost every home has some type of garden attached to the property. It may be a vegetable garden, in which one plants lettuce, peas, radishes, and tomatoes. It might be a flower garden, in which annuals such as tulips are planted, or in which various seeds grow into plants that bloom throughout the summer.

The small gardens which are a part of most homes are nothing in comparison to the acres and acres of gardens of mansions. Through these gardens a person can spend hours walking around different sections of roses and marigolds and gladiolous, all of which are separated by trimmed hedges. These huge gardens are places of multi-colored beauty which give the intruder a sense of peace and contentment.

Usually, in the midst of a garden there is a fountain. It might consist of a simple pool or a series of figurines spewing forth water. The cascade of water in the fountain adds to the comfort of the garden. The splashing water can soothe the wrinkles of the day from a person's life.

In the Song of Songs the enclosed garden is a sign that the bride is reserved for her bridegroom alone. The bride is like a garden to her groom; she cascades with human beauty and fidelity. She is most precious in the eyes of the groom.

Mary, the mother of Jesus, was such a bride of God. He chose her to be like an enclosed garden. He wrapped her in the perfume of his grace. Other than Jesus, he made her the most faithful person to ever walk the earth. God gave to Mary the fountain of life, Jesus the Christ.

Like Mary, God calls all people to fidelity. Those who are baptized in the fountain of living water and are incorporated in the body of Christ, the Church, are entrusted with a mission of faithfulness to their baptismal promises. God anoints them with the Holy Spirit and seals them with his love. Together all baptized people form the bride of Christ, who awaits the return of the groom at the end of time. While they wait, God's people are to be living water, gushing with the words and works of Jesus, the fountain of salvation.

Meditation: In what ways is your life like a garden, made up of a variety of good words and good works?

Prayer: God of gardens, once you created a special place called Eden and placed there the crown of your creation—man and woman. You made of Mary, the mother of Jesus, an enclosed garden, where fidelity and obedience to your word were planted. Form us into the image of Jesus; open our ears to hear his word and give us strength to put it into practice. Give us the fidelity of Mary, his mother, that we might share in the fountain of eternal life. We ask this through our Lord Jesus Christ, your Son, who lives and reigns with you and the Holy Spirit, one God, for ever and ever. Amen.

32. The Blessed Virgin Mary, Mother and Teacher in the Spirit
Parent-Teacher

Scripture: The foreigners who join themselves to the LORD, ministering to him,

Loving the name of the LORD,
and becoming his servants
. . . Them I will bring to my holy mountain
and make joyful in my house of prayer;
. . . For my house shall be called
a house of prayer for all peoples.

(Isa 56:6-7)

Mass: Prov 8:17-21, 34-35 or Isa 56:1, 6-7; Matt 12:46-50 or John 19:25-27

Reflection: The parents of a child are the first teachers of the child. The mother may have first place, since she begins to teach the child while she carries it in her womb. However, from the moment of birth, the child is taught with words and by example, and learns quickly.

While both parents share in this teaching capacity, each shares it in a slightly different manner. The mother nourishes the child from her own body. This gift of life-sustaining milk is one which the father cannot share. He may be able to hold a bottle of formula for the child and observe as he or she sucks its nourishment, but he cannot share in this in the same way as the mother.

Likewise, the mother cannot offer the type of life-sustaining support that the father can give. A man shares a different type of love with his son or daughter. He lifts up, holds, and embraces the child in a unique way. Fatherhood is different from motherhood.

While one parent can successfully raise a child and substitute for the other parent, no man can give to the child the unique quality of motherhood, and no woman can give to the child the unique quality of fatherhood.

Mary, the mother of Jesus, is honored as a parent and a teacher. As a parent, she carried the Christ in her womb and nourished him at her breasts. As a teacher, she taught him the truths of his ancestors and formed him in the ways of God. Throughout this endeavor, she was aided by Joseph, her husband, who offered a father's love to Jesus.

From Mary people can learn how to welcome Jesus into their hearts and nourish and care for him in the poor, the sick, and the suffering of the world. From Mary people can learn how to teach others how to study the great deeds of God in the past, listen to the teaching of Jesus, and observe the activity of God in the lives of people today.

Meditation: Identify ways that you have functioned as a parent (either mother or father) and as a teacher of the ways of God.

Prayer: God our Father, you call all people to come to your house of prayer, where you welcome them with a father's love. You give them Mary, the mother of Jesus, as an example of the motherly love that you have for all your people. Through the gift of the Holy Spirit you teach them obedience to your word. Make us faithful ministers of your word. Give us a greater love for your name. Bring us to the holy mountain, where you live and reign with our Lord Jesus Christ, your Son, and the Holy Spirit, one God, for ever and ever. Amen.

33. The Blessed Virgin Mary, Mother of Good Counsel
Counselor

Scripture: When the time for Pentecost was fulfilled, they were all in one place together. And suddenly there came from the sky a noise like a strong driving wind, and it filled the entire house in which they were. And they were all filled with the holy Spirit (Acts 2:1-2, 4).

Mass: Isa 9:1-3, 5-6 or Acts 1:12-14, 2:1-4; John 2:1-11

Reflection: A counselor is a person who offers advice or guidance to another person. In high school and college a counselor guides a student in making choices for classes. A marriage counselor helps a couple work through a problem or offers suggestions as to how the parties might enhance their marriage. In a court, a counselor is a trained professional, who represents his or her client in the face of the law.

In the New Testament the supreme counselor is the Holy Spirit, who is God's special gift to his people after the resurrection of Jesus. The Holy Spirit is often referred to as an Advocate, a legal term for defense attorney. However, the word has other connotations, such as spokesperson, mediator, intercessor, comforter, and consoler.

Sometimes the Holy Spirit is referred to as the Paraclete, a teacher, a witness, one who renders judgment on the world and represents the new presence of Jesus after his resurrection. The Holy Spirit, then, is the Counselor, who guides the Church until Jesus' return in glory.

Mary, the mother of Jesus, is often referred to as the mother of good counsel. Indeed, from the first moment of the conception of Jesus in her womb, she was overshadowed by the power of the Most High, the Holy Spirit. As a mother and teacher, she offered guidance to the Son of God. She taught him how to listen to God's word and to obey it. Mary prepared her Son for the fullness of the anointing with the Spirit, which he received at his baptism in the Jordan.

The Spirit which overshadowed Mary and anointed Jesus and was poured out on the apostles continues to guide the members of the Church today. In Baptism, every person is immersed in the Spirit-filled waters. In Confirmation, every person is sealed with the gifts of the Spirit. Pentecost continues as the Church, the body of Christ, changes and calls for conversion in the lives of all of her members.

Meditation: Recently, what guidance or counsel have you received from the Holy Spirit? Explain.

Prayer: God our counselor, once you led your people from Egyptian slavery to desert freedom. You gave them kings and prophets, who were entrusted with the task of counsel. In the fullness of time you sent your only-begotten Son, born of the Virgin Mary. Through his suffering and death he taught us the ways of your wisdom and promised the gift of the Holy Spirit. Continue to send the Holy Spirit in our lives with the force of a strong driving wind. Fill us with an eagerness to discern your will in our lives, and give us the strength to do it. We ask this through our Lord Jesus Christ, your Son, who lives and reigns with you and the Holy Spirit, one God, for ever and ever. Amen.

34. The Blessed Virgin Mary, Cause of Our Joy
Joy

Scripture: Sing and rejoice, O daughter Zion! See, I am coming to dwell among you, says the LORD (Zech 2:14).

Mass: Zech 2:14-17 or Isa 61:9-11; Luke 1:39-47 or John 15:9-12

Reflection: "Joy" is a common three-letter word which is used to describe an emotion which gives pleasure to a person. "Joy" can refer to satisfaction, gladness, delight, happiness. A person who is filled with "joy" usually rejoices. Keats said it best: "A thing of beauty is a joy for ever."

Mary is a cause of "joy." Because she consented to conceive the Son of God in her womb and to share her flesh with him in the wonder of the incarnation, she has given the world great "joy" in the person of the redeemer.

Jesus was not only God's gift to the world, but he was also the fulfillment of God's promise to dwell with people. Jesus was the enfleshment of God; he was God in human form. People rejoice in the gift of salvation brought by God through his Son, born of the Virgin Mary.

"Joy" is one of the characteristics of the followers of Jesus. Particularly, it is heralded during the Easter season as the resurrection of Jesus is celebrated. The whole earth is called upon to rejoice in the gift of new life given by God through Jesus. But even Lent, the most solemn season of the liturgical year, does not eliminate all joy. Christians realize that their preparation to renew their baptismal promises is itself a type of joy in the Risen One.

Advent is filled with the joy of the expectation of the return of the Lord and the celebration of his first appearance in history as an infant. Christmas continues the joy of the incarnation, the great mystery of God coming to live with his people.

Throughout Ordinary Time people share the joy of redemption. They learn from Mary the meaning of joy, the excitement of watching God at work in their lives. Because Mary permitted God to work freely in her life, she became a joy for ever to her Creator and a cause of joy for others. When any follower of Christ permits God to continue the process of conversion in his or her life, that person cannot but help to sing and rejoice. To God he or she is a joy for ever.

Meditation: What causes you to be joyful? How has God's activity in your life given you joy?

Prayer: God of joy, you came to live with your people in the flesh and blood of your only-begotten Son, Jesus. He became man in the womb of the Virgin Mary, who bore him with the purest love. Your Church rejoices in so great a gift. Give us a greater reverence for your name. Set our hearts on fire with an enthusiasm for your will. Enable us to rejoice in your activity in our lives as we wait in joyful hope for the coming in glory of our Lord Jesus Christ, who lives and reigns with you and the Holy Spirit, one God, for ever and ever. Amen.

35. The Blessed Virgin Mary, Pillar of Faith
Blessedness

Scripture: A woman from the crowd called out and said to [Jesus], "Blessed is the womb that carried you and the breasts at which you nursed." He replied, "Rather, blessed are those who hear the word of God and observe it" (Luke 11:27-28).

Mass: Jdt 13:14, 17-20; Luke 11:27-28

Reflection: The word "blessed" is best understood as "happiness." A "blessed" person is one who has received a divine favor and is happy about the gift. To call another "blessed" is to attribute a beatitudinal quality to that person. One who is "blessed" has been favored by God.

An unnamed woman in a crowd declares the womb that carried Jesus and the breasts at which he nursed to be blessed. In other words, Mary, the mother of Jesus, is praised for the divine favor of being the mother of the Son of God. She was favored by God from the moment of her own conception and prepared by God for this special role in salvation history.

But the Lukan Jesus, while not degrading the blessedness of his mother, points toward a greater blessedness: hearing the word of God and observing it. It is not the biological relationship in which God has an interest. What is more important is an attentiveness to God's word and a demonstration of how one lives that word or puts it into practice.

Luke, then, models Mary after this understanding of "blessed." Mary is happy because she responds to God's word and conceives the Christ in her womb. She obeys the Father's will and listens attentively as her Son is presented in the Temple and, later, as he teaches the teachers. Mary is portrayed as the first "Christian"; that is, she demonstrates how one follows Christ. Hearing the word of God and practicing it is what makes her happy or blessed.

Hearing the word of God and observing it is what makes her a pillar of faith. She believes. She trusts her God even when she does not understand all of the events that surround her. According to Luke, she remains faithful to Jesus through his death and resurrection. She joins the apostles in the upper room to await the completion of her Son's work—the gift of the Holy Spirit.

Such blessedness is a quality that is offered to every person who willingly follows in the footsteps of Jesus. Every Christian can be called blessed. All he or she has to do is to hear the word of God and observe it. The word echoes from the pages of the Bible; it resounds from the documents of the Church; it echoes in the halls of learning. It can be observed by conversion, a radical change in one's life, which focuses on those values which really matter. As a person struggles with the word of God and the change in lifestyle which it implies, he or she gradually discovers authentic happiness.

Meditation: Identify three ways that you have heard the word of God and observed it. For each of these, how have you experienced happiness?

Prayer: Blessed are you, Lord our God, king of the universe. Like rain from the heavens, you shower your word upon your people. You call us to conversion and a change of heart. Give us the attentiveness of Mary, the mother of Jesus. Give us the strength to make the changes in our lives that will please you. Keep us strong in faith. We ask this through our Lord Jesus Christ, your Son, who lives and reigns with you and the Holy Spirit, one God, for ever and ever. Amen.

36. The Blessed Virgin Mary, Mother of Fairest Love

Fair

Scripture: I bud forth delights like the vine,
 my blossoms become fruit fair and rich.
Come to me, all you that yearn for me,
 and be filled with my fruits.

(Sir 24:17-18)

Mass: Sir 24:17-21; Luke 1:26-38

Reflection: A person who is said to be fair is one who is beautiful, attractive, pleasing to look at. A fair person is one who is a feast for the eyes of another.

Mary, the mother of Jesus, is often referred to as the fairest one. This means that she is beautiful, attractive, and pleasing in the eyes of all.

Mary is fair because she was bathed in God's grace from the moment of her conception. God filled her with his own eternal life and prepared her to be the purest of mothers for his only-begotten Son, Jesus. Like a rivulet turning into a stream, Mary was drenched with the special gifts of God.

She is fair because she was the first to share in the gift of the Holy Spirit. She kept the covenant of her people and observed the Law so that she shone forth like the first streaks of dawn in the dark, eastern sky. The Holy Spirit overshadowed her, protected her, and made her radiant in the eyes of her Creator. After her Son's death and resurrection, she joined the apostles in the upper room to experience again the strong, driving wind of the Spirit of God, as he re-created the people on the earth.

Finally, Mary is fair because she, like a vine that blossoms and brings forth fruit fair and rich, conceived the Son of God in her own womb and gave birth to him in the wonder of the incarnation. From Mary, the fairest vine, blossomed the Savior of the world.

Mary's beauty is a feast for the eyes of God. Her fairness is an example for the followers of her Son. God is not interested in physical appearance, but God's concern is for the acceptance of his gifts of grace, Spirit, and eternal life. The person who accepts these gifts is fair in God's eyes.

Meditation: In what ways are you a feast in the eyes of God? In other words, how are you fair, like Mary?

Prayer: God of the fair, you send your gifts of wisdom and grace, like a rivulet that turns into a stream, to those who stand with open hands before you. From the depths of our lives you cause blossoms to bud into the finest fruit of the Holy Spirit. May we always drink deeply of your teachings, carefully observe your covenant, and, like Mary the mother of your Son, be counted as beautiful in your presence. We ask this through our Lord Jesus Christ, who lives and reigns with you and the Holy Spirit, one God, for ever and ever. Amen.

37. The Blessed Virgin Mary, Mother of Divine Hope
Tree of Hope

Scripture: "I have struck root among the glorious people,
in the portion of the LORD, his heritage.
Come to me, all you that yearn for me,
and be filled with my fruits;
You will remember me as sweeter than honey
better to have than the honeycomb."

(Sir 24:12, 18-19)

Mass: Sir 24:9-12, 18-21; John 2:1-11

Reflection: In an age that has awakened to a great concern for the environment, many people are busily planting trees or saving forests in a race against time. Other people are trying to cut down on the amount of trash that goes into landfills every day by recycling. Some work to enact laws that will establish minimum standards of cleanness for car and factory emissions in order to keep the air safe for human consumption.

These actions among others give people hope that they can save the planet on which they live. Probably the most concrete sign of hope is the planting of a tree. A small sapling is carefully planted in the earth, in which it takes root. People plant trees to commemorate birthdays, anniversaries, weddings, and special holidays. The growing tree reminds them of the special occasion as well as the hope-filled moment during which they planted it.

Mary, like a tree, represents hope. She, like her ancestors, hoped to see the day of the Messiah, the one who would deliver her people from oppression and domination. In hope she conceived the Son of God in her womb, and with more hope gave birth to him in the miracle of the incarnation.

Her assumption into heaven made her the sign of hope for all God's people. Just as she was raised to share in the glory of Christ's resurrection, so too all people hope to share in the same new life. As people make their pilgrimage upon the earth, they can look to Mary as an example of hope.

She is like a great tree which spreads its graceful branches toward the heavens. People can stand in the shade of her hope. They can follow the branches of her fidelity. They can learn a lesson about how strong and permanent hope can be.

Meditation: Besides a tree, what other signs of hope are there? To which of these do you look for strength?

Prayer: God of hope, once you planted many trees in the garden of Eden and commanded the first man and woman not to eat from the tree of the knowledge of good and evil. When they ate its fruit, they lost all hope of ever seeing your face. In Mary hope for the human race crystallized as she give birth to your Son, Jesus the Christ. On the tree of the cross he gathered all people under the branches of your love and instilled in them the hope for eternal life. May we always eat of the fruit of the cross and attain the new life that Jesus has bestowed on us. We ask this through our Lord Jesus Christ, your Son, who lives and reigns with you and the Holy Spirit, one God, for ever and ever. Amen.

38. Holy Mary, Mother of Unity
Unity

Scripture: There is one God.
There is also one mediator between God
and the human race,
Christ Jesus, himself human,
who gave himself as ransom for all.
(1 Tim 2:5-6)

Mass: Zeph 3:14-20 or 1 Tim 2:5-8; John 11:45-52 or John 17:20-26

Reflection: In what was most likely an early Christian creed, people professed that there is one God. This belief was nothing new; it came directly from the daily prayer of every Jew: "Hear, O Israel! The LORD is our God, the LORD alone!" (Deut 6:4).

However, the next part of the profession of faith is what was new. Jesus was declared to be the one mediator between God and people. Jesus was the go-between, the one who occupied the intermediate place between God and people.

Jesus, the eternal Son of God, accomplished his role as mediator by becoming human and giving himself as a ransom for all. His death on the cross was the price he paid for salvation.

Mary is named the mother of unity because in her womb the union of Jesus' nature as God and his nature as man took place. The womb of the Virgin of Nazareth was where the unity between God and people was first conceived.

By stretching out his arms in death, Jesus gathered all the scattered children of God into one. He made them his body, so that never again would God become separated from people. So close is the unity between God and people that God sealed it with the gift of the Spirit.

Today, many people work against the unity of the body of Christ. There are those who prefer to do their own thing rather than to support the work of the whole Church. It seems that every person knows more than the collective wisdom of the whole body.

Some people draw lines of division which are based on the color of a person's skin or the economic bracket into which one fits or the neighborhood to which one belongs. Other people put up fences or walls; they draw boundaries or set limits.

Mary, as the mother of the unity of the divine and human natures of Christ, stands as an example of what the people of God, the body of Christ, can be. Jesus' will is that all people be united among themselves and with God, their Creator. To work against this prayer represents a failure to understand the creed that Christians profess.

Meditation: During the past week, what did you do to foster unity in the Church? What did you do to hinder unity in the Church?

Prayer: One God, from the beginning of time you have willed that your people be united with you. In one great act of love, you sent the one mediator, Jesus, who gave himself as a ransom for all people. In the womb of Mary, his mother, he united divinity and humanity in one person and prayed that all people might share in this unique harmony as members of his body. Through the movement of your Holy Spirit, bring all people together in your Church. Erase the lines that divide them from each other. Make all men and women realize the great hope to which they are called in Christ Jesus, your Son, who lives and reigns with you and the Holy Spirit, one God, for ever and ever. Amen.

Ordinary Time: Section 3

39. Holy Mary, Queen and Mother of Mercy
Option A: Intercessor

Scripture: Queen Esther, seized with mortal anguish, likewise had recourse to the LORD. Then she prayed to the LORD, the God of Israel, saying: "My LORD, our King, you alone are God. Help me, who am alone and have no help but you, for I am taking my life in my hand. Save us by your power, and help me, who am alone and have no one but you, O LORD," (Esth C:12, 14-15, 25).

Mass: Esth C:12, 14-15, 25, 30; John 2:1-11

Reflection: An intercessor is a person who intervenes between parties in an attempt to help them reconcile their differences. One who intercedes may do so by negotiations. However, in a religious context, an intercessor is one who prays to God for another. He or she petitions or entreats God to bestow a particular favor upon another or upon a group of people.

Queen Esther was considered to be an intercessor between God and her people, the Jews. When they were threatened with destruction at the hand of the wicked counselor, Haman, Esther interceded on their behalf. Her prayer of petition asked God not to let this evil deed take place and to give her the words she needed to appeal to her husband, King Ahasuerus, to reverse Haman's decision.

Like Queen Esther, Mary, the mother of Jesus, is considered to be an intercessor. This means that because of her special place in the events of salvation she prays to God on behalf of people. Mary brings the prayers and petitions of people to God, and asks that God grant these favors.

While Mary's role is unique as an intercessor, all people who follow Jesus can function as intercessors for each other. In other words, because every Christian has been baptized into the body of Christ, each one has an obligation to pray for the needs of every other member of the same body. During the Liturgy of the Hours and the celebration of every sacrament and blessing, the whole

Church offers general intercessions on behalf of herself and her members.

During moments of private prayer, individual Christians remember to pray for each other, especially members of their families, those who suffer from illness, those preparing for travel, those who face particular problems, etc. People petition God for help and strength. They ask God to help others know God's will and to practice it in their lives. This type of personal prayer, as well as community prayer, asks God to look mercifully upon his people during their time of need.

Meditation: When have you most recently functioned as a public intercessor within the body of Christ? For whom did you pray? When have you most recently functioned as a private intercessor? For whom did you pray?

Prayer: God of Queen Esther, you alone are God, King, and Ruler of the earth. Through our incorporation in the body of Christ, you have made it possible for us to make prayers and supplications to you in time of need. Put the necessary words in our mouths that we might be able to open our lips in prayer for others. Fill us with your Holy Spirit that we might know how to petition you. May we join our prayers to those of Mary, the mother of our Lord Jesus Christ, who lives and reigns with you and the Holy Spirit, one God, for ever and ever. Amen.

39. Holy Mary, Queen and Mother of Mercy
Option B: Mercy

Scripture: By grace you have been saved through faith, and this is not from you; it is the gift of God; it is not from works, so no one may boast. For we are his handiwork, created in Christ Jesus for the good works that God has prepared in advance, that we should live in them (Eph 2:8-10).

Mass: Eph 2:4-10; Luke 1:39-55

Reflection: God has always offered grace to people. In fact, God makes the first move and waits for a response. God offers people the gift; if they accept it and believe, they are saved. It is pure gift; it is undeserved. Furthermore, it cannot be earned as a reward for good deeds. People have nothing to do with initiating it; this is solely left up to God. All they can do is to accept the free gift.

This tremendous gift of God is often referred to as God's mercy. God has pity on people and looks upon them with divine compassion. God smiled upon his handiwork when he sent his only-begotten Son to the earth. Jesus was born of Mary, upon whom God bestowed a special favor—he preserved her from sin from the moment of her conception.

In other words, God's mercy took flesh in the person of Jesus of Nazareth. By giving birth to him in the miracle of the incarnation, Mary can be called the mother of mercy.

Through the waters of Baptism all people are called to share in God's mercy. Not only do they stand in the stream of God's grace, but they share God's compassion and care with each other.

During a time of crisis, one person who listens attentively to another is offering the other the merciful understanding of God. After a disagreement, a husband and wife who bestow unlimited forgiveness upon each other are sharing God's merciful love for the world. Even children can be taught to be kind to each other and reveal the mercy of God.

Mary experienced God's mercy in a special way. However, through the suffering, death, and resurrection of Jesus, God has made it possible for everyone to accept his constantly offered free gift of grace and mercy.

Meditation: During the past week, in what ways have you extended the mercy of God to others?

Prayer: God of infinite mercy, when your people sinned and turned away from you, you did not abandon them. Through the prophets you called them to conversion of heart. Through the suffering, death, and resurrection of Jesus, you offered them a new life of faith through grace. Look upon us in your compassion and strengthen our will for doing good. Enable us to extend to everyone we meet the mercy that you have given to us. We ask this through our Lord Jesus Christ, your Son, who lives and reigns with you and the Holy Spirit, one God, for ever and ever. Amen.

40. The Blessed Virgin Mary, Mother of Divine Providence
Providence

Scripture: When the wine ran short [during the wedding in Cana in Galilee], the mother of Jesus said to him, "They have no wine." [And] Jesus said to her, "Woman, how does your concern affect me? My hour has not yet come." His mother said to the servers, "Do whatever he tells you" (John 2:3-5).

Mass: Isa 66:10-14; John 2:1-11

Reflection: When one speaks about "providence," one is usually referring to God's guidance or care. For believers, God is conceived of as the power that sustains and guides the universe and human destiny; that is, God provides for the future. As long as God is around, both the world and people have a future.

Because Mary gave birth to the Son of God, Jesus, she can rightly be called the mother of divine providence. As the mother of Jesus, Mary is also the mother of God, who cares for and guides the world and all the people in it. In the beauty of the incarnation, Mary gave birth to the One who insured a future for the whole universe. Jesus referred to this future as the kingdom of God.

Every day people experience God's providence, his kingdom. To wake from sleep and rise from the darkness of night to see the birth of a new day and the first streaks of the dawn is a glimpse of God's magnificent care and guidance. The ability to solve a problem by thinking it through carefully and by talking to another person about it in order to get another viewpoint can be an experience of God's providence. As one shares a friendly smile with another at work or lunch with a fellow employee or dinner with family and friends, God's kingdom is made present. The future is assured.

Like the servers at the Cana wedding celebration, people have to be willing to trust that God is taking care of the future. When

Mary instructed the waiters to do as Jesus told them, she was being a model of trust in God's providence. Even though the hour of Jesus' passion, death, resurrection, ascension, and gift of the Spirit had not yet come, God, nevertheless, took care of his people. The wedding is a sign of God's covenant with people; it is a marriage sealed in the blood of Jesus which will last for ever.

Meditation: In what ways have you experienced God's provident care and guidance?

Prayer: Provident God, through the paschal mystery of Jesus, born of the Virgin Mary, you renewed your covenant with your people. You never cease to care and guide them through their pilgrimage of life. Fill us with a greater trust that we might recognize your presence in our midst. Ensure our future by granting us a share in the eternal wedding feast of the kingdom, where you live and reign with our Lord Jesus Christ, your Son, and the Holy Spirit, one God, for ever and ever. Amen.

41. The Blessed Virgin Mary, Mother of Consolation

Consolation

Scripture: The spirit of the Lord God is upon me,
  because the LORD has anointed me;
He has sent me to bring glad tidings to the lowly,
  to heal the brokenhearted,
To proclaim liberty to the captives
  and release to the prisoners,
To announce a year of favor from the LORD
  and a day of vindication by our God,
  to comfort all who mourn;
To place on those who mourn in Zion
  a diadem instead of ashes
To give them oil of gladness in place of mourning,
  a glorious mantle instead of a listless spirit.
          (Isa 61:1-3)

Mass: Isa 61:1-3, 10-11 or 2 Cor 1:3-7; Matt 5:1-12 or John 14:15-21, 25-27

Reflection: While a husband or wife is undergoing serious surgery, members of the family and friends often will gather in the waiting room of the hospital and console the one who is not having the surgery. Likewise, when a loved one dies, family and friends gather for a funeral and offer their condolences to the nearest relative of the deceased in attempts to console him or her. On a day-to-day basis, parents console a child who falls down and scrapes a knee or loses a little league baseball game or doesn't get the part in the school play or doesn't get asked to the prom.

When one person consoles another, he or she offers comfort and tries to eliminate the grief, the sorrow, the sense of loss, or the trouble of another. This may be done with carefully chosen words, a friendly smile, a loving embrace, or true presence. The purpose of consolation is to let the suffering person know that he or she is not alone in sorrow and that others are there to assist and to support him or her in that time of need.

God is the greatest of all consolers. When God's people were trapped in slavery in Egypt, God let them know through Moses that he was one with them in their suffering. When they were taken as captives to Babylon, God promised them a new leader who would be anointed with the Spirit. This leader would have a particular mission to the afflicted, those who mourned.

In the fullness of time, God's consolation took flesh in the person of Jesus of Nazareth. Born of the Virgin Mary, Jesus preached the consolation of God. He brought good news to the poor and healing to the brokenhearted. Those trapped in self-made prisons were offered freedom. Those held captive by prestige and wealth were offered liberty.

Jesus' mission was particularly to the suffering, who received a crown instead of slavery. Those without hope could look to the suffering, crucified, and risen Christ for their strength. God's consolation was made flesh in his only-begotten Son.

Because she was the mother of the Savior, the Consoler, Mary is rightly called the mother of consolation. Mary experienced all the sorrow, brokenheartedness, and agony of any other human being, especially in the death of her Son. Because of her own experience, she is able to console her brothers and sisters in the Church. She experienced the consolation of the resurrection of Jesus, and, in turn, she offers consolation to all the afflicted.

Meditation: In what ways are you a consoler? During the past year, whom have you consoled? What was the occasion?

Prayer: God our consoler, when we are brokenhearted, you send us the good news of your kingdom. When we are imprisoned in sin, you offer us the release of forgiveness. When we mourn, you crown us with gladness and wrap us in your grace. Continue to anoint us with your Spirit. Through the prayers of the Virgin Mary, the mother of consolation, enable us to reach out in comfort to all our brothers and sisters in need. We ask this through our Lord Jesus Christ, your Son, who lives and reigns with you and the Holy Spirit, one God, for ever and ever. Amen.

42. The Blessed Virgin Mary, Help of Christians
Help

Scripture: War broke out in heaven; Michael and his angels battled against the dragon. The dragon and its angels fought back, but they did not prevail and there was no longer any place for them in heaven. The huge dragon, the ancient serpent, who is called the Devil and Satan, who deceived the whole world, was thrown down to earth, and its angels were thrown down with it. Then I heard a loud voice in heaven say:
"Now have salvation and power come,
    and the kingdom of our God
    for the authority of his Anointed.
For the accuser of our brothers is cast out,
    who accuses them before our God day and night.
They conquered him by the blood of the Lamb
    and by the word of their testimony."
(Rev 12:7-11)

Mass: Rev 12:1-3, 7-12, 17 or Gen 3:1-6, 13-15; John 2:1-11

Reflection: One of the great messages of Judaism and Christianity is that God never abandons his people. Once God enters into a covenant relationship with people, God never gives up on them. God continuously seeks out people, reconciles them to himself, and invites them into the kingdom.

The Hebrew Bible (Old Testament) is one continuous narrative of God's rescue of people. It begins with the creation of the world for the benefit of human beings. The first story of creation is immediately followed by the account of the first sin and God's promise that he would not abandon his creation.

Noah and his family saw the rainbow as the sign of the covenant between them and God that never again would God destroy the earth with a flood. Abraham and Sarah conceived Isaac as the child of the promise of descendants as numerous as the stars of the sky or the sands of the seashore. Moses spoke with God face to face as he accepted the covenant that included the Promised Land.

God's unwillingness to abandon his people is found in the judges who ruled his people and in the kings who followed the judges. The prophets preached God's presence by reminding the people of God's word and mighty deeds throughout their history.

The greatest sign of God's union with people is Jesus, born of the Virgin Mary. He was the incarnate presence of God. Flesh and blood like anyone else, Jesus was the fulfillment of God's promise to never abandon his people.

In coded language the Book of Revelation speaks of the help that God is always giving to his people. In times of trial, God is there. Michael, whose name means "Who can compare with God?" or "Who is like God?", demonstrates that God always defends his faithful people. Through Jesus, the Anointed One, God has established his kingdom for his people.

Because Mary gave birth to the Son of God, the One who never ceases to help his followers, she is called the help of Christians. Anyone who faithfully follows her Son can be assured of her help and the assistance of her Son.

Meditation: During the past week, how has God helped you?

Prayer: God our help, when your people were held captive in slavery, you did not abandon them; rather, you sent Moses to lead them to freedom. When they were taken as prisoners of war to Babylon, you raised up Cyrus, king of Persia, who released them. Through your prophets you renewed your covenant always to be with your people. Jesus, your Son, born of the Virgin Mary, brought the good news of your salvation and power. Through his word and deeds he established your kingdom. With his blood he conquered evil and made it possible for all people to be your sons and daughters. May we always know your presence in our lives and experience the help of your Anointed One, Jesus Christ, who lives and reigns with you and the Holy Spirit, one God, for ever and ever. Amen.

43. Our Lady of Ransom
Ransom

Scripture: The high priest Joakim and the elders of the Israelites, who dwelt in Jerusalem, came to see for themselves the good things that the LORD had done for Israel, and to meet and congratulate Judith. When they had visited her, all with one accord blessed her, saying:
"You are the glory of Jerusalem,
    the surpassing joy of Israel;
    You are the splendid boast of our people.
With your own hand you have done all this.
    You have done good to Israel,
    and God is pleased with what you have wrought.
May you be blessed by the LORD Almighty
    forever and ever!"
And all the people answered, "Amen!" (Jdt 15:8-10).

Mass: Jdt 15:8-10; 16:13-14; John 19:25-27

Reflection: Usually the word "ransom" is understood to refer to an amount of money demanded or paid for the redemption of a person held in captivity. In order for parents to free their child from a kidnapper, they may be forced to pay a ransom. Hostages in foreign countries are held for a ransom. When a ransom is demanded, it means that a price has been placed on a person's life.

The Hebrew Bible (Old Testament) Book of Judith portrays the nation of Israel in captivity before Holofernes, general-in-chief of the forces of Nebuchadnezzar, king of the Assyrians. Judith, a widow, with a well thought-out plot lures the general into his own tent, where she cuts off his head. Thus, Judith frees Israel from Holofernes' siege. The risk of her own life is the ransom.

Mary, the mother of Jesus, is another woman who served as a ransom in the history of salvation. By agreeing to be the mother of the Christ before being united in marriage to Joseph, her husband, she risked being stoned to death. In the miracle of the incarnation, she gave the world its redeemer. Jesus ransomed the whole world through his suffering, death, and resurrection. The price was his life.

Today, followers of Jesus continue the ransoming process. Anytime one person is willing to spend a few extra minutes listening to the sufferings of another, he or she frees the other from his or her burdens. Lifting a hand in service at a local soup kitchen can free one person from hunger. Working for economic justice can ransom another from poverty.

The price is always some sharing of life. Mary shared her life with God. Jesus shared his life with all people. Followers of Jesus are called to continue to ransom each other, like Judith, who freed her people from the siege of Holofernes.

Meditation: In what ways have you ransomed someone during the past week?

Prayer: God of Judith, you made your servant the glory of Jerusalem and the surpassing joy of Israel. You chose Mary to be the mother of Jesus, who ransomed the human race through his suffering, death, and resurrection. Give us the courage of Judith and the strength of Mary. Help us to serve our brothers and sisters in need. May you be blessed, Almighty Lord, Father, Son, and Holy Spirit, one God, as you live and reign for ever and ever. Amen.

44. The Blessed Virgin Mary, Health of the Sick
Healed Infirmities

Scripture: It was our infirmities that he bore,
our sufferings that he endured,
While we thought of him as stricken,
as one smitten by God and afflicted.
But he was pierced for our offenses,
cursed for our sins,
Upon him was the chastisement that makes us whole,
by his stripes we were healed. . . .
If he gives his life as an offering for sin,
he shall see his descendants in a long life,
and the will of the LORD shall be
accomplished through him.

(Isa 53:4-5, 10)

Mass: Isa 53:1-5, 7-10; Luke 1:39-56

Reflection: A person who suffers from infirmities does so due to human weakness and fraility. Anyone who is weak of mind, will, or character can be said to be infirm. Age, disease, or mental disorders may cause infirmities.

The infirm are in need of healing, which is usually accomplished at the hands of trained, professional persons. For diseases, one usually is cared for by a doctor or a specialist in a particular medical field. If it is a mental problem from which a person suffers, a psychologist, psychiatrist, or counselor may be the source of healing. Those who are infirm due to age find care from family, nursing homes, or other specialized institutions.

While human weakness cannot be eliminated, it has been redeemed and made holy. Jesus, the Son of God, born of the Virgin Mary, showed people the value, dignity, and beauty of suffering. By becoming man, he shared in all human infirmities. He experienced the human condition in its entirety: birth, growth, struggle, suffering, death.

The value of infirmity is that it reminds people that they are not powerful, but human. The dignity of suffering is that it does not erode humanity, but it enhances it. The beauty of one's infirmities exists in the gradual transformation into the image of Jesus which they bring about.

God, the Father of Jesus, does not take pleasure in human infirmities, but God has made them holy. By becoming man, Jesus showed people how to live, how to suffer, and how to die. He did the will of God and taught others how to permit God's will to be done in them.

Instead of devaluing human suffering, Christians see it as a remembrance of their powerlessness before the might of God. Followers of Jesus see their infirmities as giving greater depth and meaning to their human dignity. And, they find beauty in suffering as they are conformed to the image of Jesus. By viewing infirmities these ways, followers of Jesus discover the healing touch of God.

Meditation: How do you view human infirmities? In what ways has God healed you during the past year?

Prayer: God of Jesus, your only-begotten Son, born of the Virgin Mary, became man and experienced all our human infirmities. He raised suffering from the depths of despair to the heights of glory and endowed it with value, dignity, and beauty. Enable us to touch the depths of our own humanity in order that we might experience your healing. May your will always be accomplished in our lives. We ask this through our Lord Jesus Christ, your Son, who lives and reigns with you and the Holy Spirit, one God, for ever and ever. Amen.

45. The Blessed Virgin Mary, Queen of Peace
Peace

Scripture: The people who walked in darkness
have seen a great light;
Upon those who dwelt in the land of gloom
a light has shone. . . .
For a child is born to us, a son is given us;
upon his shoulder dominion rests.

> His dominion is vast
> and forever peaceful,
> From David's throne, and over his kingdom,
> which he confirms and sustains
> By judgment and justice,
> both now and forever.
>
> (Isa 9:1, 5-6)

Mass: Isa 9:1-3, 5-6; Luke 1:26-38

Reflection: Since the first two primitive people banded together in order to protect themselves and founded the first tribe, people have sought peace with each other. Usually, peace is hoped for in the supreme authority of a ruler, such as a king, a queen, a prime minister, or a president. Because of the leader's dominion, he or she is supposed to bring about peace.

While the ideal remains, the fact of the matter is that peace is not a reality. The supreme authority of one person usually goes with the dominion of another person. Peace may be achieved with a fence across the back yard, a hedgerow, or some other means of establishing the boundaries of one's property in order to keep some people in and others out.

One nation continues to threaten the sovereignty of another nation by multiplying conventional and nuclear weapons, by taking hostages, by holding political prisoners, by patrolling borders. These actions may not trigger war, but the absence of war is not peace.

Within nations there may be a facade of peace in the economic arena as one corporation secretly attempts to take over another through stock purchases and other manipulative operations. People end up fighting for their jobs and their investments. Some call this type of peace a sign of a healthy economy.

Authentic peace comes from God. It is not found in darkness, but in the light. It is not made by adults, but is brought about by a child. This is the irony of God's peace: a child shoulders dominion, and this authority is forever peaceful.

This dream-child of the prophet Isaiah was made flesh in the birth of Jesus of Nazareth. He not only preached peace, but he lived it in his own life. Born of the Virgin Mary, he suffered and died, but his Father raised him to new life. Peace, according to Jesus, is absolute trust in the power of God. To predicate all power of God is to imply that people have none. And when people recognize that they have no power, they can do nothing other than live in peace.

Mary, the mother of Jesus, is often referred to as the queen of peace. By consenting to God's will, she acknowledged God's sovereignty and her own lowliness. She permitted God's dominion in her life and, thus, experienced the peace of God.

Today, opportunities abound for peacemaking. Every person must acknowledge God's kingdom and power, and his or her own powerlessness. Then, with God's reign firmly established, peace can become a reality, because people will no longer be vying for power. Peace is the absence of power.

Meditation: During the past week, in what ways have you effectively established peace by relinquishing your power and acknowledging God's sovereignty?

Prayer: God of peace, through the preaching of Jesus, your servant and your Son, you established your kingdom of peace. The Virgin Mary was the first to hear your word and to do your will; thus, she accepted your peace and relinquished the power of the world. When we are tempted to walk in our own light, remind us of the true light of Christ. When we are tempted to seek our own power, remind us that only you are supreme. When we seek our own paths to peace, guide us in the ways of Jesus, who lives and reigns with you and the Holy Spirit, one God, for ever and ever. Amen.

46. The Blessed Virgin Mary, Gate of Heaven
Awaiting the Bridegroom

Scripture: "The kingdom of heaven will be like ten virgins who took their lamps and went out to meet the bridegroom. Five of them were foolish and five were wise. The foolish ones, when taking their lamps, brought no oil with them, but the wise brought flasks of oil with their lamps. Since the bridegroom was long delayed, they all became drowsy and fell asleep. At midnight, there was a cry, 'Behold, the bridegroom! Come out to meet him!' " (Matt 25:1-6).

Mass: Rev 21:1-5; Matt 25:1-13

Reflection: Wisdom and foolishness are often juxtaposed in order to emphasize the importance of being wise over being foolish. Wisdom is as simple as common sense; in the terms of the Matthean parable, it is taking a supply of oil for one's lamp. Foolishness is the inability to plan ahead; in the terms of Matthew's parable, it is not bringing along a supply of oil.

The focus is on the oil that keeps the lamps burning. The oil is a metaphor for one's life. The wise person is the one who has stored up good deeds and is prepared to meet the bridegroom, Christ, when he comes in glory. The foolish person is the one who has kept putting off any righteous works and is not prepared to meet the groom when he arrives.

Mary, the mother of Jesus, is portrayed as a wise virgin. She listened to the word of God and willingly said yes to God's will. She, greeting the bridegroom in her womb, nourished him in the depths of her heart, and gave him to the world for its salvation. She was ready to greet him when he came; she remains vigilant for his coming again in glory.

As a model of vigilance and wisdom, the Virgin Mary can be referred to as the gate of heaven. She shows people the way to salvation. With a mother's love she points toward her Son, the bridegroom, and exhorts those who follow him to do so with plenty of oil in their flasks for their lamps.

Every person baptized into the body of Christ can drink of this wisdom and share it with others. When the chains of those in poverty are broken, gates of economic freedom swing open. When the walls of racism are toppled, the door of the equal human dignity of every person is opened. People who give an honest day's work for an honest day's wage provide an entrance for truthfulness as a way of life.

Many times during the day the cry is heard, "Behold, the bridegroom!" The wise have plenty of light and are ready to meet him.

The foolish find themselves looking for oil, while the groom goes into the wedding feast and the door is locked.

Meditation: Recently, in what way have you opened a door for someone? Do you consider yourself wise or foolish? What kind of oil do you have for your lamp?

Prayer: God of the kingdom, once you gave the world its bridegroom, your Son, born of the Virgin Mary. After his suffering, death, and resurrection, you promised that he would return. While we await his coming again in glory, fill us with an eagerness for wisdom. Guide us with the gift of your Holy Spirit. Help us to know your will and to do it that we might have our lamps burning brightly for the bridegroom, our Lord Jesus Christ, your Son, who lives and reigns with you and the Holy Spirit, one God, for ever and ever. Amen.

Appendix

Lectionary Scripture Texts from
Common of the Blessed Virgin Mary

Outside Easter Season

Gen 3:9-15, 20
Gen 12:1-7
2 Sam 7:1-5, 8-11, 16
1 Chr 15:3-4, 15-16; 16:1-2
Prov 8:22-31
Sir 24:1, 3-4, 8-12, 19-21
Isa 7:10-14
Isa 9:1-6
Isa 61:9-11
Mic 5:1-4
Zech 2:14-17

Rom 5:12, 17-19
Rom 8:28-30
Gal 4:4-7
Eph 1:3-6, 11-12

Matt 1:1-16, 18-23
Matt 2:13-15, 19-23
Luke 1:26-38
Luke 1:39-47
Luke 2:1-14
Luke 2:15-19
Luke 2:27-35
Luke 2:41-52
Luke 11:27-28
John 2:1-11
John 19:25-27

During Easter Season

Acts 1:12-14
Rev 11:19; 12:1-6, 10
Rev 21:1-5

Rom 5:12, 17-19
Rom 8:28-30
Gal 4:4-7
Eph 1:3-6, 11-12

Matt 1:1-16, 18-23
Matt 2:13-15, 19-23
Luke 1:26-38
Luke 1:39-47
Luke 2:1-14
Luke 2:15-19
Luke 2:27-35
Luke 2:41-52
Luke 11:27-28
John 2:1-11
John 19:25-27

Other Scripture Texts from
Lectionary for Masses of the Blessed Virgin Mary

Gen 22:1-2, 9-13, 15-18
Gen 28:10-17
Exod 3:1-8
Num 24:15-17
Ruth 2:1-2, 8-11; 4:13-17
Isa 11:1-5, 10
Mic 5:1-4
Zech 9:9-10

Rom 5:12, 17-19
Rom 8:28-30
Rom 12:9-16
1 Cor 15:20-26
1 Cor 15:54-57
Eph 1:3-6, 11-12
Col 1:21-24
Heb 5:7-9

Matt 1:18-23
Matt 13:54-58
Mark 3:31-35
Mark 6:1-6
Luke 24:44-53

Index of Scripture Texts